IMAGES of America
CAPE CORAL

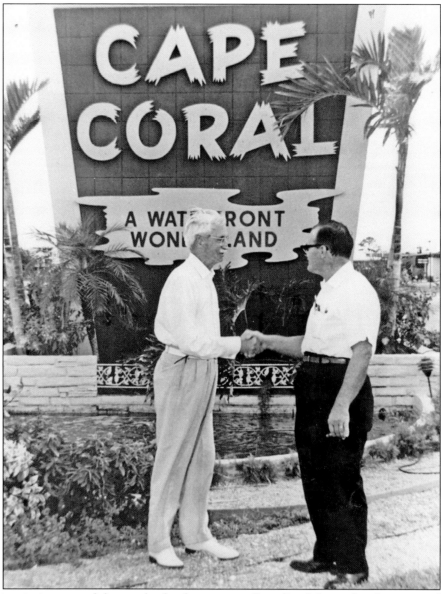

This iconic sign greeted thousands of early visitors to Cape Coral. It stood at the corner of Cape Coral Parkway and Del Prado Boulevard and promised a "Waterfront Wonderland." This slogan went on to become a major marketing tool for the salesmen selling the Cape Coral dream. The famous sign is long gone, and its current whereabouts are a mystery. The man on the right is restaurant owner Willy Gruetzenbach. (Cape Coral Historical Museum.)

ON THE COVER: In 1962, the Amphibicar made an appearance in Cape Coral. Passersby were agog as the white convertible drove right off the beach and into the water. Two nylon propellers on the back powered the strange vehicle. Marketing managers with the Gulf American Land Corporation reportedly bought two Amphibicars to take potential customers on a once-in-a-lifetime voyage. This picture shows Peggy Tanfield, Don Brownfield, and a Gulf American salesman out for a joyride. (Cape Coral Historical Society.)

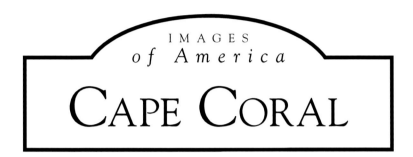

IMAGES of America
CAPE CORAL

Chris Wadsworth, Anne Cull, and the
Cape Coral Historical Society

Copyright © 2009 by Chris Wadsworth, Anne Cull, and the Cape Coral Historical Society
ISBN 978-0-7385-6771-6

Published by Arcadia Publishing
Charleston, South Carolina

Printed in the United States of America

Library of Congress Control Number: 2009920843

For all general information contact Arcadia Publishing at:
Telephone 843-853-2070
Fax 843-853-0044
E-mail sales@arcadiapublishing.com
For customer service and orders:
Toll-Free 1-888-313-2665

Visit us on the Internet at www.arcadiapublishing.com

Chris: To my father and mother, Doug and Ellen Wadsworth, for teaching me a love of books and reading—and for being wonderful parents.

Anne: To my dear husband Fred—for all of the love and support he has shown to me in all of my endeavors.

Contents

Acknowledgments		6
Introduction		7
1.	Early Settlers: Life on Harney Point Road	9
2.	Rosen Brothers: Developers with a Dream	19
3.	Aviation: Cape Coral from the Sky	37
4.	Early Amenities: Places to Go, Things to Do	43
5.	Rose Garden: The Famous Cape Coral Gardens	61
6.	Celebrities: Hollywood Glamour on the Cape	71
7.	Waterfront Wonderland: Life on the Water	83
8.	Daily Life: Becoming a City	93
About the Organization		127

ACKNOWLEDGMENTS

First and foremost, thank you to the many fine families, individuals, and organizations—including the *Cape Coral Daily Breeze*, the Cape Coral Police Department, the Cape Coral Fire Department, and the Schroder family—who donated so many fascinating and historic photographs to the Cape Coral Historical Museum. Nearly all photographs in this book come from the museum's archives, which would not have been possible without the generosity of the community.

Thanks to Maura Granger-Bohl, who spent countless hours scanning the photographs used in this project. Her help—and that of her patient husband, Jeff Bohl—proved to be immeasurable.

Thanks also to Lindsay Harris and Luke Cunningham, our editors at Arcadia Publishing, for their consistent good-natured help as we developed this book.

Thanks to Paul Sanborn, the Cape's official historian, for his early support of this book project and his wonderful firsthand knowledge of the city's development, which he so willingly shared.

Thanks to Pat Molter Emerson, whose pioneer family roots proved to be invaluable in writing about the Cape's earliest settlers.

Thanks to Chuck and Barbara Hostetler, Carolyn Zenoniani, Suzanne Miranda, Chris Schroder, and Alice Hunt for the copious research and assistance that went into this book.

Thanks also to Val Everly, Todd Everly, Amy Williams, the Elkhart Historical Society, Victor Zarick, the Southwest Florida Museum of History, and the State Library and Archives of Florida for providing additional photographs used herein.

Thanks to the City of Cape Coral for its support of the Cape Coral Historical Society and the Cape Coral Historical Museum.

Finally, thanks to the citizens of Cape Coral—old and new—who continue to contribute to this community's unique story.

INTRODUCTION

A horrible massacre—at least a dozen men killed!

It is certainly not the claim to fame or marketing slogan that any community would choose. That could have been Cape Coral's fate had not some entrepreneurial brothers intervened.

But let's not get ahead of ourselves.

In July 1839, a band of 160 warriors from the Seminole tribe, including the famous Billy Bowlegs, attacked a garrison of U.S. soldiers camped at Harney Point. That is near the location where today's Cape Coral Parkway and Del Prado Boulevard meet. Historians say 13 men were killed, while another 14—including Lt. Col. W. S. Harney—escaped into the Caloosahatchee River.

As the decades unrolled and the community of Fort Myers began to grow across the water, the main thing people knew about the land that would become Cape Coral is that it was the site of the infamous Harney Point Massacre.

In the late 1800s and early 1900s, a few brave pioneers began moving west from North Fort Myers and setting up homesteads in the northern Cape. The government granted large tracts of land, rough-and-tumble cabins and homes were built, and farming began.

A few citrus crops dotted the peninsula here and there, but cattle farming was the main industry in the Cape's early days, as cattle roamed freely through much of the area's woodlands and scrublands.

Life in the area called Redfish Point—due to the great redfish fishing along its shores—continued slowly for the next half-century.

Then, in the late 1950s, two brothers began cutting deals with the cattle companies and landowners in the Cape, buying up hundreds of acres of land. The men were Jack and Leonard Rosen of Baltimore, Maryland, and they had a plan.

They intended to literally carve a new city out of the sandy soil and thick foliage that covered the Cape—and what a city it would be: beaches, sunshine, stores and attractions, and as many canals as the famed city of Venice. Indeed, the "Waterfront Wonderland" they envisioned would become an advertising slogan for the Rosens.

The duo had run a successful hair care product company, using the relatively new medium of television to pitch their products and enlisting celebrities as spokespeople. Many consider these efforts the forerunners of today's infomercials.

The ingenious brothers figured if the technique worked for shampoo, then similar techniques would work for land. With their Gulf American Land Corporation, the Rosens began carving out canals, clearing land, building homes, and marketing, marketing, marketing.

Brochures and postcards were mass mailed to chilly northerners touting the wonders of the new Cape Coral. Sales teams were dispatched to major northeastern cities like Boston, Syracuse, and Hartford as well as European cities. Model homes were given out as prizes on game shows such as *Concentration* and *The Price is Right*. Celebrities like Bob Hope, Anita Bryant, and Hugh Downs were invited to visit, giving the burgeoning community a glamorous, Hollywood-like air.

On the ground, restaurants and motels were opened, the famous Surfside Restaurant and Nautilus Motel being the first. They were soon followed by a yacht club, a country club and golf course, and the famed Cape Coral Rose Gardens. It was everything a community would need to attract visitors and convince them to buy homes or invest in land for their future.

Planeloads of passengers flew into Southwest Florida and made their way on buses to Cape Coral. There they would board single-engine airplanes for edge-of-your-seat flights over the sparse land as pilots pointed out properties and the sites of future amenities.

Salesmen would put on the hard sell, convincing would-be customers that now was the time to buy. If a potential buyer seemed to hesitate, another salesman would rush into the room and stick a pin in another property. Buy now or miss out on the opportunity of a lifetime—that was the message.

It was a thrilling time in Cape Coral, and eventually thousands upon thousands of northerners (and a few Floridians too) bought into the Rosen brothers' dream.

The first major hiccup in Gulf American's business plan came in 1967, when the *Wall Street Journal* published a story that accused Gulf American and the Rosens of fishy practices—switching lots on naive customers, dirty sales tricks, and making promises that did not live up to reality. That was coupled with an adversarial Florida governor and new oversight on the state's real estate industry.

The company faltered, was bought out, went through bankruptcy, and was reborn. But by this time, the cows were out of the barn, so to speak. Cape Coral was no longer just the largest planned residential development in the United States, it was a fully functioning community, and indeed, by 1970, local voters chose to incorporate. The City of Cape Coral was born.

Over the next decade, Cape Coral would continue to grow, as new businesses moved into the city, new schools were built, and the population exploded. Many of the early land purchasers from the 1960s were retiring, and they were moving south to the Cape to make their long planned "Waterfront Wonderland" dreams come true. By the mid-1980s, Cape Coral became the largest city in Lee County, surpassing its older cousin across the river. It is a trend that continues to this day.

The purpose of this book is to celebrate these early years—the trials and tribulations, the saints and the sinners, the rural lives and the boom years—that came together to form a city with one of the most unique histories of any place in North America.

Some people will tell you Cape Coral is so new, it does not have a history. Hah! Now you can tell them otherwise.

One
EARLY SETTLERS
LIFE ON HARNEY POINT ROAD

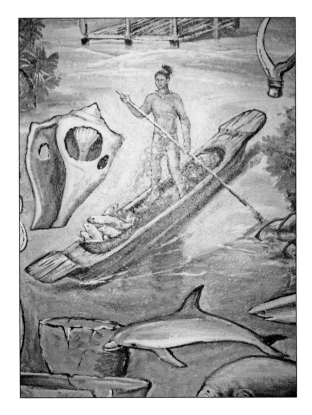

While many people think Cape Coral's history started in the late 1950s, it actually goes back much further. Native Americans, including the long-gone Calusa Indians, once populated the land that is now Cape Coral. Evidence including arrowheads, beads, and pottery has been found in the area. This mural from the Cape Coral Historical Museum was painted by Carrie Keller and shows scenes from early Native American life in the region.

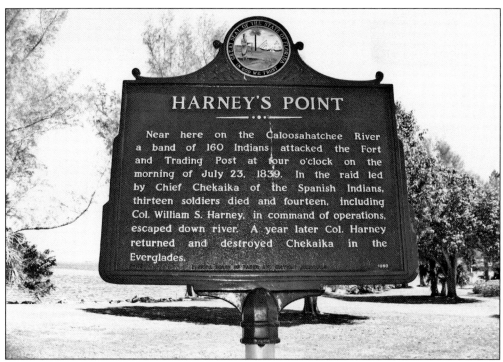

By the early 1800s, American settlers had moved into many regions of northern Florida, and the Native Americans' time of dominance was waning. A series of wars were fought, and one of the most celebrated incidents happened in what is now Cape Coral. A memorial plaque stands near the site. It reads: "Harney's Point—Near here on the Caloosahatchee River a band of 160 Indians attacked the Fort and Trading Post at four o'clock on the morning of July 23, 1839. In the raid led by Chief Chekaika of the Spanish Indians, thirteen soldiers died and fourteen, including Col. William S. Harney, in command of operations, escaped down the river. A year later Col. Harney returned and destroyed Chekaika in the Everglades." Scholars debate whether these facts are all accurate, but all agree that the attack reignited hostilities.

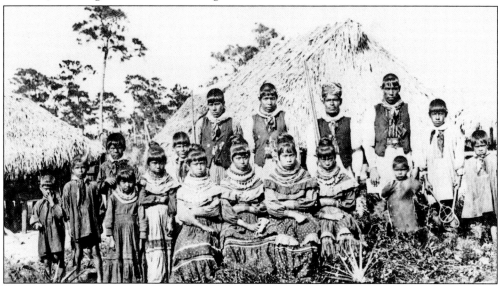

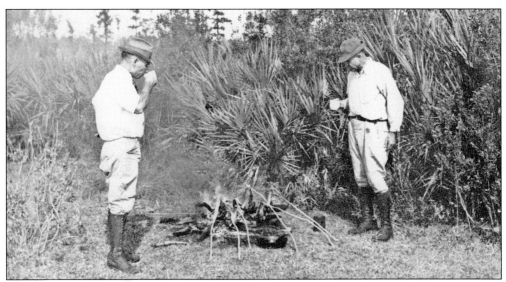

Camping and fishing in the Cape were some of the early activities of white settlers who came from more developed areas across the river. Homesteaders started moving into the thick woods north of the Caloosahatchee River in the late 1800s and early 1900s. The area that would become Cape Coral was known by the unusual name "Hungry Land." The origin of this moniker is unknown. Building hardscrabble homes and farms, these intrepid pioneers led a rough and isolated life miles from the hubbub of Fort Myers.

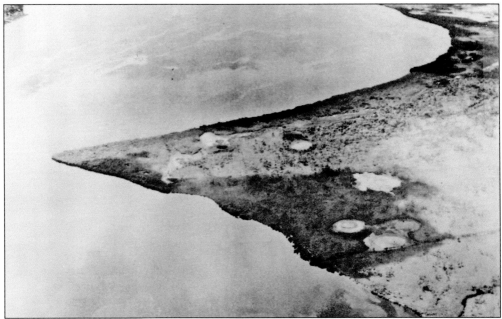

In the winter of 1904, Dr. Franklin Miles arrived in Fort Myers for a short visit. His family owned Miles Laboratories, the producers of Alka-Seltzer. While fishing and hunting near the Cape, he inquired about growing vegetables in the area. Locals told him crops other than citrus would not flourish here because of the climate. Nonetheless, Dr. Miles began to experiment with vegetable gardens and, in 1908, purchased his first parcel of land near the site of the present-day Cape Coral Bridge.

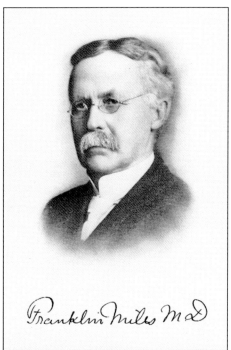

Franklin Miles farmed muck, planted experimental gardens, and started a school for local farmers. Buying land at 75¢ an acre, Dr. Miles eventually owned more than 1,700 acres of land in Cape Coral near what is now the downtown area—from the Cape Coral Bridge to the yacht club. This area was long known as Redfish Point due to the good fishing off its shores.

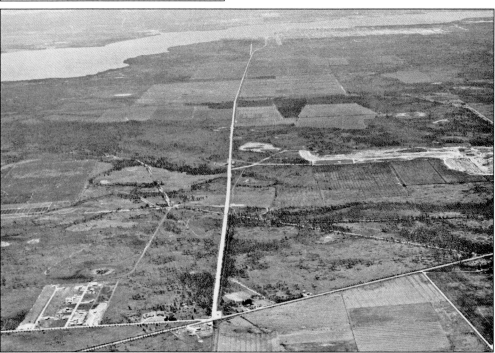

This aerial photograph shows Harney Point Road, which would become busy Del Prado Boulevard. It shows just how empty Cape Coral was prior to the start of major development in the late 1950s. Another major landowner in the early Cape was the Matlacha Cattle Company, which owned 25,000 acres. Cattle farmers used much of the wide-open land, and early residents recall that it was common to see cows roaming across local roads.

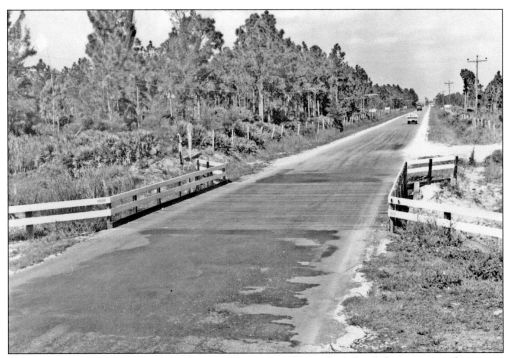

This photograph also shows the old Harney Point Road. Nearby is land that was once known as Heifer Heights due to the cattle farming in the area. Today it is where one finds Nicholas Parkway and the Cape Coral Police Department. Eventually the Gulf American Land Corporation bought up 114 square miles of land from local landowners. The company that would develop Cape Coral into a modern city paid anywhere from $165 to $2,000 per acre.

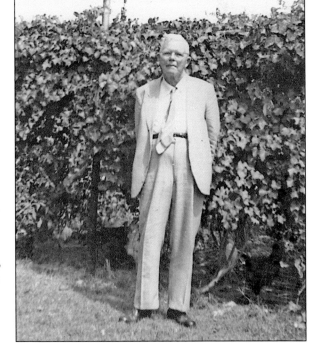

William T. Belvin was a schoolteacher and a self-ordained minister from Georgia. After Belvin lost his first wife, he took his two children, Eloise and Beaman, and moved to Southwest Florida. He set up his homestead on land granted to him by the federal government. The property was located near present-day Trafalgar Parkway. Belvin Grade was the roadway that led to their very primitive homestead.

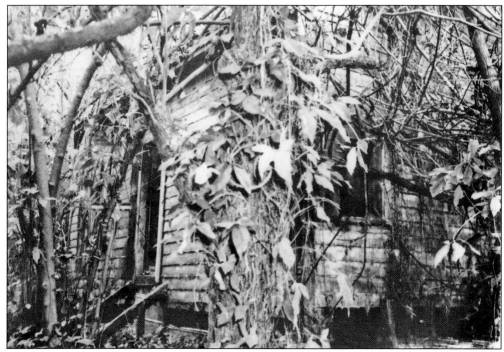

The house was a chickee, or thatched roof hut, and the living conditions were so bad that Eloise moved to Fort Myers and lived with a local minister and his wife. Belvin worked as a farmer and raised hogs. He kept a cultivated garden, and the property was dense with guava, mango, and orange trees. In 1950, the homestead was sold, but much of the area was left undeveloped. In 1988, construction workers building a new school uncovered the remains of the Belvin cabin still intact.

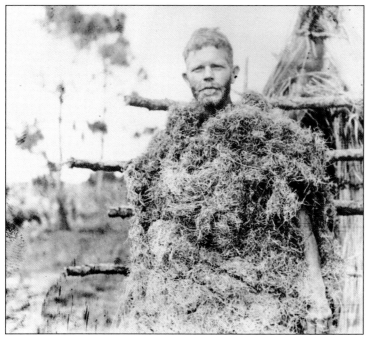

In 1929, Belvin gained great fame for pulling what was apparently an elaborate publicity stunt for a Fort Myers newspaper, the *Tropical News*. He set out to prove that someone could be dropped naked into the wilds of Florida and survive for a year. He did just that, eating fish, shellfish, fruits, and small game. He made himself clothing from animal hides and plants. He emerged a year later, reportedly weighing 10 pounds more than when he went into the woods.

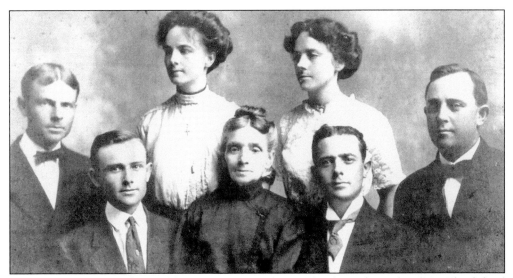

Brothers Jacob and Hoge Blackley arrived in Southwest Florida in the early 1920s. The federal government granted Jacob 160 acres in northern Cape Coral. Their homestead was across from William Belvin's property, near present-day Southwest Twentieth Avenue. They used the land primarily for growing citrus, which did well in Cape Coral's subtropical climate.

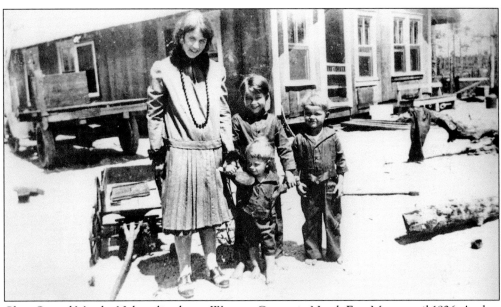

Chris Sr. and Martha Nelson lived near Weavers Corner in North Fort Myers until 1926. At that time, Chris applied for and received 160 acres from the federal government for homesteading north of Pine Island Road. Chris moved Martha and their two children to the property but continued to work in North Fort Myers.

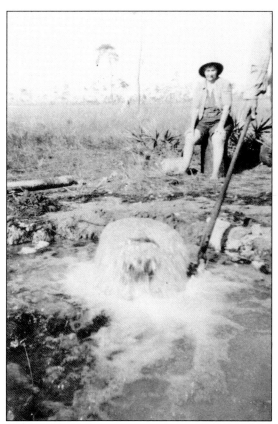

Martha spent most of her time alone, but recalled the neighbors stopping by on Sunday with covered dishes. After Chris's death, Martha married J. P. Nielsen and moved away from the homestead. Years later, she returned and lived in the house near Pine Island Road until her death. Into the 21st century, Martha and Chris's children and grandchildren continued to live on the property.

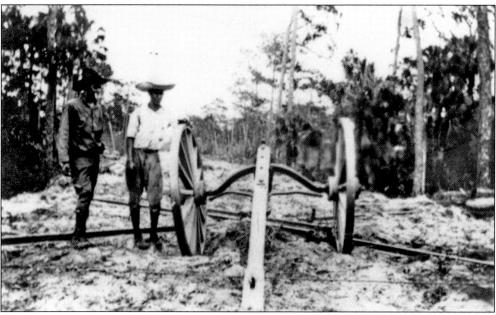

This photograph from 1925 shows just how difficult life in the early Cape could be. The road these men are standing on—if it can be called a road—is Pine Island Road. The men are Elam Underhill (left) and Ezra Corbitt (right).

The Corbitts were an early family in the region. Ruben Corbitt had property near the current headquarters of the Lee County Electric Cooperative in North Fort Myers. In 1922, Ruben's son, Anthony "Tone" Corbitt, was granted 160 acres of land by the federal government in Cape Coral. The Corbitt homestead was a small parcel of land in the woods east of what is now the intersection of Santa Barbara Boulevard and Cape Coral Parkway. The house was a simple two-room structure with wooden shutters propped open with a stick. Horses, hogs, and chickens for market were the main source of income for the Corbitts. The horses had stalls in the barn, while the cows and pigs ran loose. The farm raised potatoes, corn, peas, and rice. After "Tone" Corbitt's death in 1931, his widow and son sold the property and moved to Fort Myers. Corbitt descendants still remain in the area today.

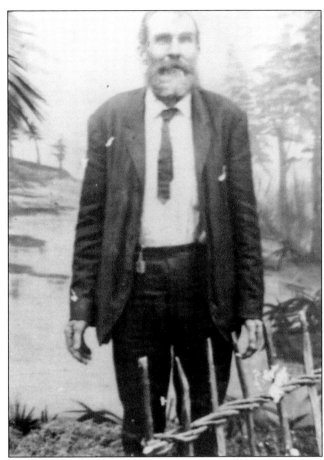

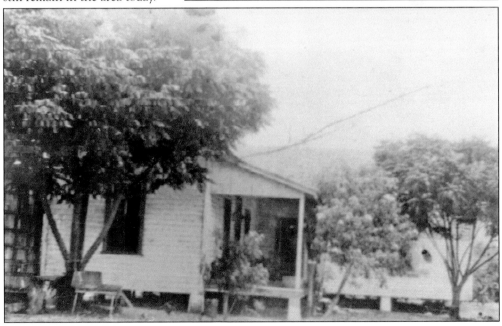

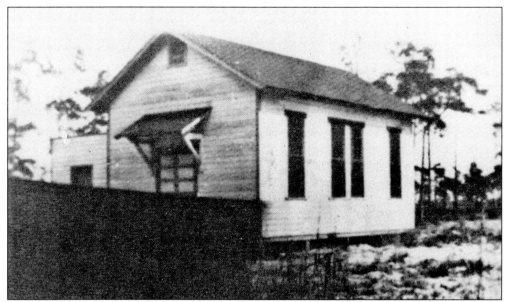

Jacob Blackley deeded 2.5 acres of land to the Lee Board of Instruction in 1926. There, the first school in the Cape was built for $1,448, which included "two toilets." It was a one-room school for six grades and had about 12 students. It was known as the Matlacha School, and Wilma Pierce was its first and only teacher. The school closed in 1927, and children were sent to the new J. Colin English Elementary School in North Fort Myers. The short-lived Cape school was on Molter Grade Road, now Chiquita Boulevard, near where Trafalgar Elementary School is today.

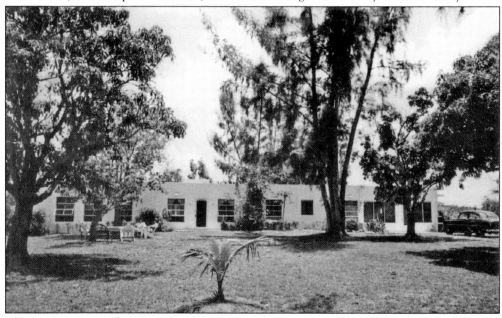

The first known motel in Cape Coral sat near the intersection of Pine Island Road and Chiquita Boulevard in the northern Cape. It was built in 1946 and was named the Ranch House Motel. It primarily served northerners who came to the area in the winter in order to fish on Pine Island. Today the motel site is the location of the Coral Ridge Cemetery. The funeral home on the property is the original motel building.

Two

ROSEN BROTHERS
DEVELOPERS WITH A DREAM

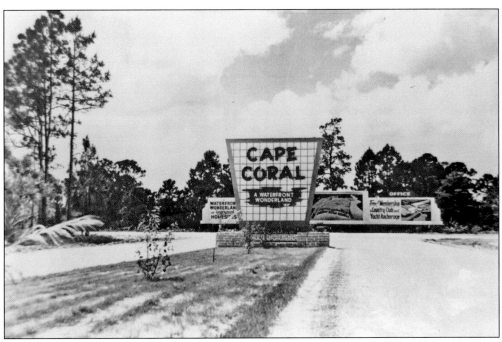

Fast-forward a few decades, and much of what is now Cape Coral was still wild scrubland. In 1957, two entrepreneurs had a vision of what this enormous parcel of land could become—a major, modern metropolitan city and home to thousands of northerners seeking a piece of the Florida dream.

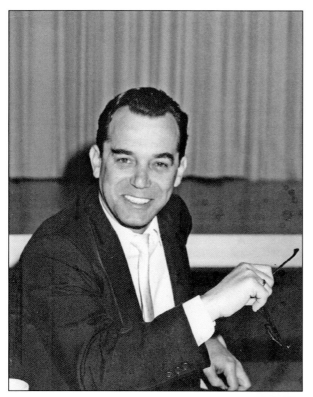

In 1950, Jack Rosen (left) of Baltimore, Maryland, was convinced that he and his brother, Leonard, could sell their Charles Antell hair products on the newly invented television. They purchased cheap airtime when stations were normally off the air and started a nationwide mail-order business. This was the start of infomercials. The Rosens used celebrities in their commercials. This method later proved successful in promoting land sales in the future Cape Coral.

The success of other land sales operations in Florida motivated Leonard (right) and Jack Rosen to get into the land business. They formed a company called Sandy Investment Company and purchased 1,724 acres on Redfish Point in July 1957. The peninsula that extended into the Caloosahatchee River was part of a tract of land owned by the estate of Franklin Miles Laboratories. The company paid $678,000.

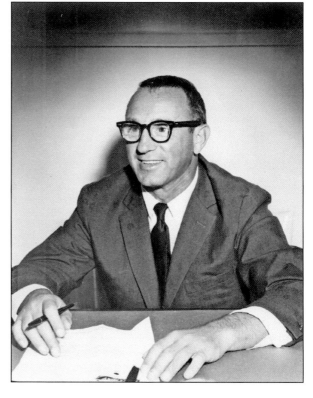

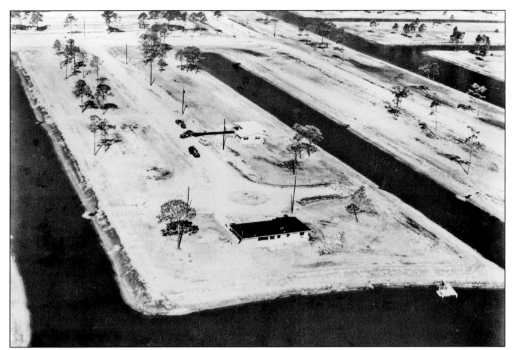

Later in 1957, their investment company became known as the Gulf Guaranty Land and Title Company, which was later renamed the Gulf American Land Corporation. Gulf American is the name used in much of this book. With their corporate structure in place, the Rosens began assembling a construction force that was soon to transform the tract of Florida pineland into home sites. These photographs from 1958 and 1959 show some of the earliest development by Gulf American—the clearing of land, the dredging of canals, the laying out roads, and the start of home building.

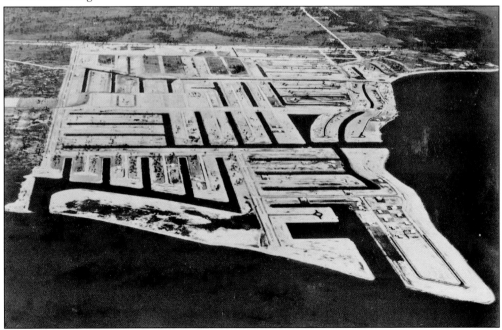

21

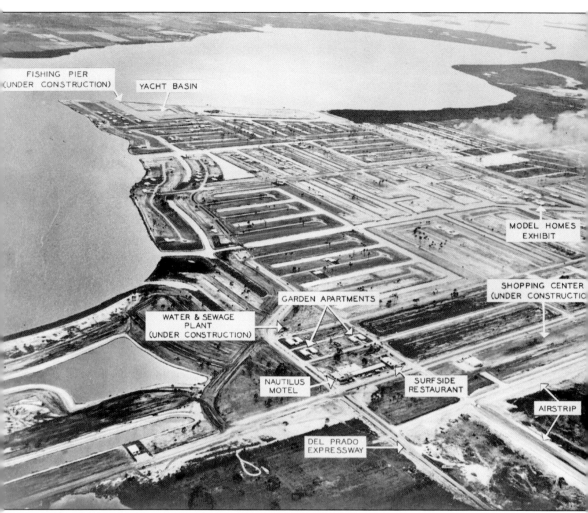

Leonard Rosen met Tom Weber in 1957 and took him to look at the Redfish Point land purchase. He convinced Weber that they were going to build a city on the site. Even though Weber was doubtful, he took on the job of chief engineer. Tom Weber's first task was building a road into the development that would be passable year-round. The only existing road was Harney Point Road, a narrow, bumpy trail that flooded during heavy rains. By October 1958, six miles had been rebuilt but not yet paved. It was renamed Del Prado Boulevard. At the same time, other crews finished 2 miles of Cape Coral Parkway. The parkway was Gulf American's northern border and ran from Del Prado to Coronado Parkway. Coronado south to the yacht basin was the initial western border.

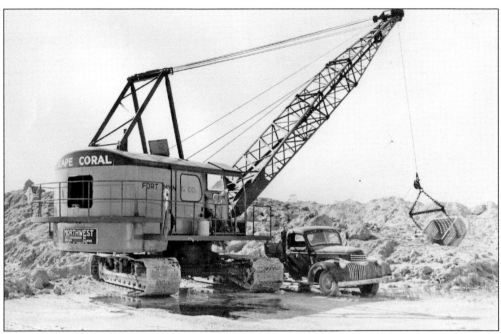

Before any dredging could begin, the area had to be cleared of the pines that had been lumbered in the 1920s to 1940s. As road building continued, construction of the yacht basin and the first canal began. Tom Weber and his crew staked out all the canals and roadways. During the first five years, all construction in Cape Coral depended on the speed of the canal dredging.

Because the excavated dirt was needed to build up the home sites, dredging continued through the night, with huge spotlights illuminating the scene. By mid-1962, the three dredges in the project were accompanied by 10 draglines. The hydraulic dredgers were floating barges that pumped out dirt in a liquid solution. The draglines were cranes that dragged gigantic buckets across the ground, picking up dirt from canal sites and dumping it on higher ground.

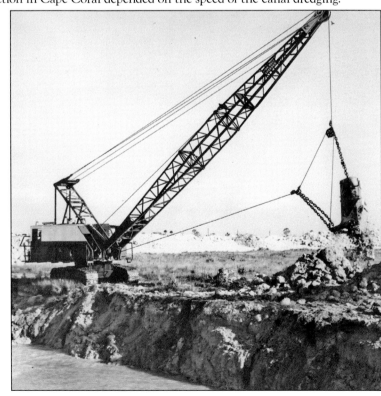

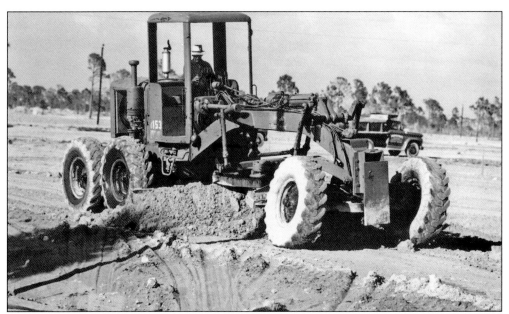

In some areas, a heavy layer of coral rock had to be blasted with explosives. Nearly 40 tons of dynamite had been used to break up the rock over a five-year period. With so much excavated material, the company did not have to buy and haul in fill dirt.

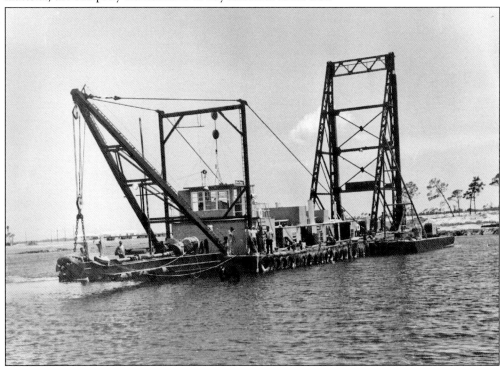

The result of five years of dredging and grading was 168 miles of canals and three basins—Bimini, Bikini, and the yacht basin. Fourteen artificial lakes were dug, and 80 miles of paved roads crisscrossed the growing development. By early 1963, Tom Weber reported that 50 million cubic yards of dirt had been dredged at Cape Coral.

In March 1958, customers with the desire to live in Florida were driven down Coronado Parkway to the river. They were shown several models built by the Duffala Construction Company and the Connie Raymond Company of Punta Gorda. These models were between Riverside and Flamingo Drives. The first home was built for Kenny Schwartz and his family. They moved into it in 1958 and were the Cape's first residents. Kenny is the man in these two photographs, and he was the general manager in charge of the development of Cape Coral. As of this writing, he is retired and living in Hollywood, Florida.

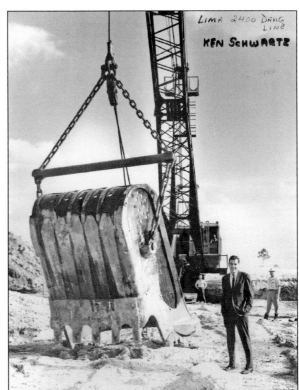

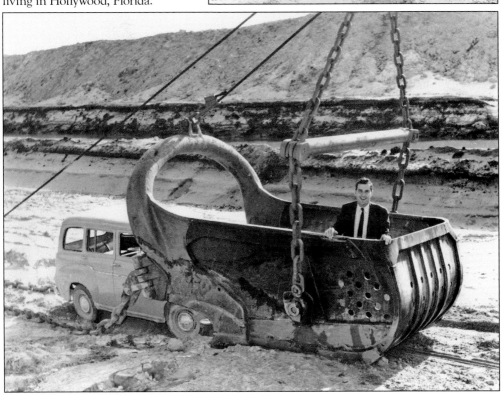

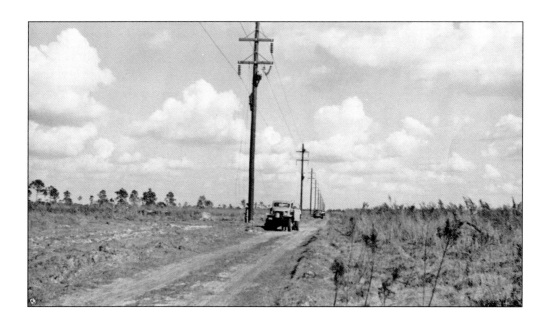

There was power in some areas of the Cape prior to the arrival of the Rosen brothers, but it needed to be greatly expanded and brought south to the new homes popping up in the southern Cape. Leonard Rosen shook hands with Homer T. Welch of the Lee County Electric Cooperative (LCEC) and promised him it would be a good investment to run electricity cables 8 miles down Del Prado Boulevard. Rosen put up $3,000 in earnest money. The wires were strung, and the first resident moved into his fully powered home in June 1958. Within a year, 24 homes were hooked up, and LCEC was turning a profit in southern Cape Coral. Rosen got his deposit back. Initially there were 17 streetlights along Del Prado Boulevard, and Kenny Schwartz would patrol them and let LCEC know when one burned out.

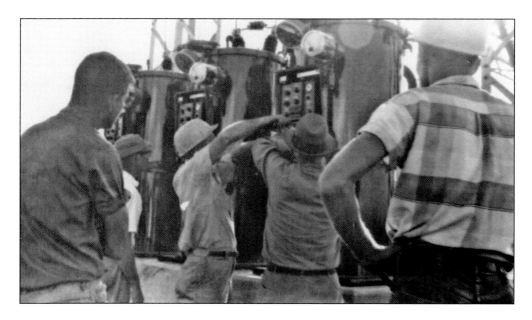

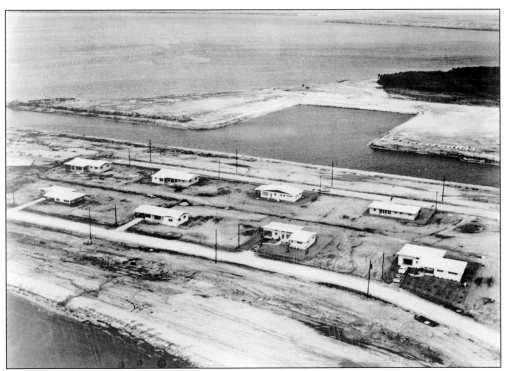

Riverside Drive and Flamingo Drive, near the yacht club, are where the first eight homes were built in Cape Coral. These homes were of a contemporary style custom tailored to the individual's taste. That meant buyers were assured that there would not be row after row of monotonous looking homes. It guaranteed high property values and luxurious neighborhoods.

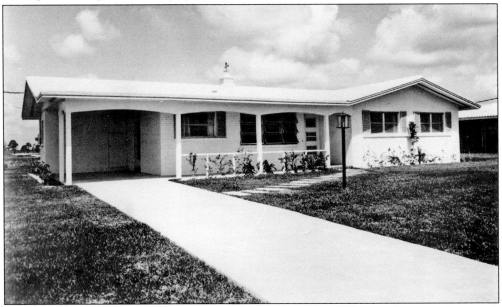

In the early 1960s, homes in Cape Coral were given out as prizes on popular game shows such as *The Price is Right*, *Queen for a Day*, and *Concentration*. Many winners kept their homes as investments or retirement properties while others sold the homes and took the cash.

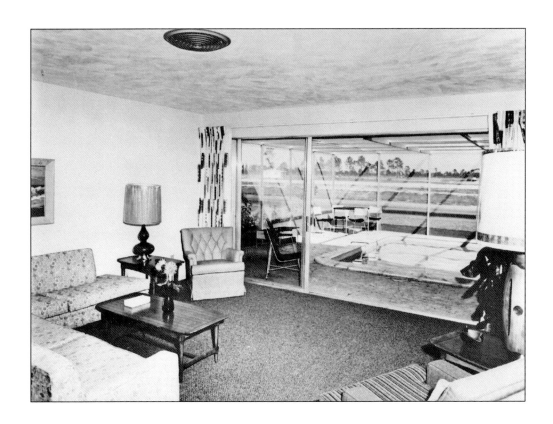

Arthur Rutenberg signed an agreement with Gulf American in 1959 to build houses. The first model home village opened on York Court at the corner of El Dorado Parkway and Coronado Parkway. These models were the Cherokee, selling for $10,990, and the Ambassador, offered for $26,250. From 1959 to the mid-1960s, Arthur Rutenberg built more than 500 homes in Cape Coral.

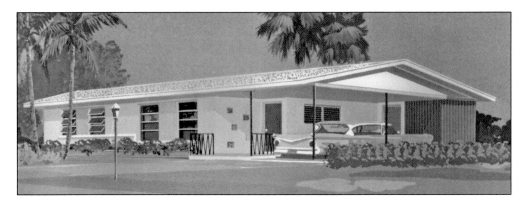

Marketing materials were an instrumental part of the Rosens' public relations campaign, as brochures and postcards were sent to potential customers across the land. "In all of Florida—No Spot More Lovely!" and "3,400 acres of Sunny Dreamland" were some of the phrases used to create an image of paradise. Homes were billed as "waterfront" and "waterview." "You can acquire a choice quarter-acre Waterview Home site for as little as $20 down and $20 monthly," read one brochure.

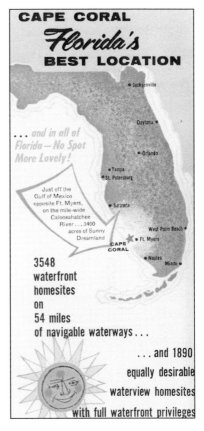

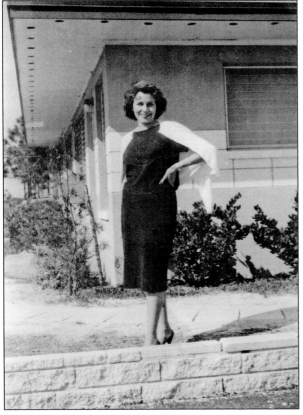

Mary Anderson Harborn was the first sales person hired by Gulf American and the only woman. She worked at the small office at Weavers Corner in North Fort Myers. In March 1958, the office was moved to a four-plex on the corner of Cape Coral Parkway and Coronado Parkway. Every morning, she stopped on her way to work to buy groceries so she could fix lunch for prospective home buyers.

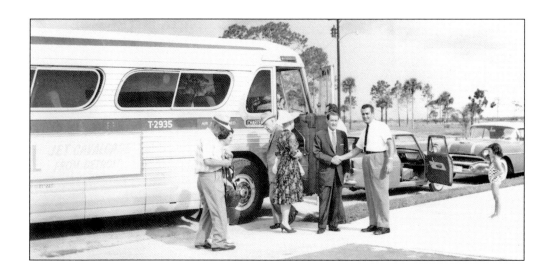

Brokers in large northern cities recruited and screened prospective buyers. Prior to a free trip to Cape Coral, the prospects deposited $500 with Gulf American, which was refunded if no sale occurred. Buyers toured the area by bus and single-engine plane. A three-day, two-night stay cost an average of $120, and the sales closure rate was 92 percent. The first buyer on record was Hank Snodgrass. These photographs show people arriving by bus for their visit to Cape Coral. Just as homebuyers in large developments do today, potential buyers could stand in front of a large map and choose from among the available home sites.

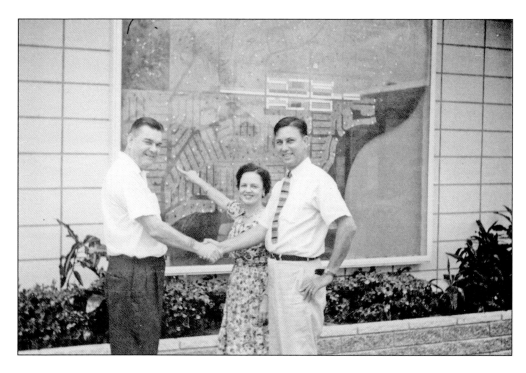

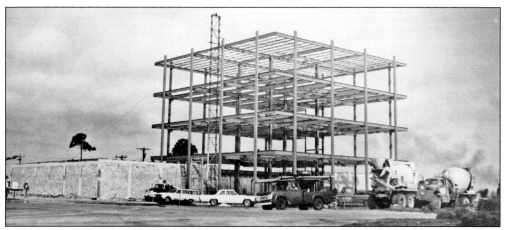

In the main Cape sales office building (seen under construction), Ed Pacelli, senior vice president of sales, had a bank of switches in his office. From there, he could listen in to any of the sales offices downstairs. This ability to eavesdrop allowed managers to make sure their commission-based salesmen were not straying too far from the Gulf American script. On the other hand, if a potential customer seemed to be waffling, a closer listening elsewhere could rush into the room, out of breath, and ask if "Lot 24" was still available, because he had a buyer. Or he would come in and stick a pin in a lot next to the one the customer was considering. These tactics were meant to make customers think they were about to miss out on a deal and pressure them to buy.

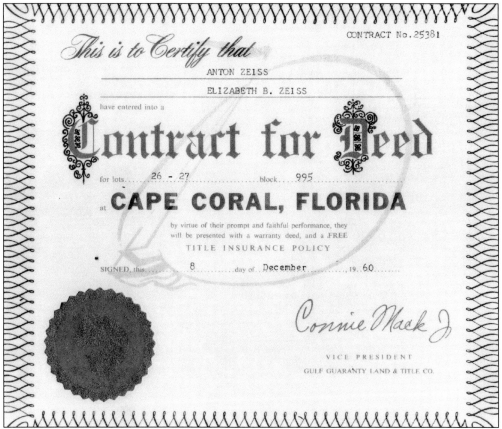

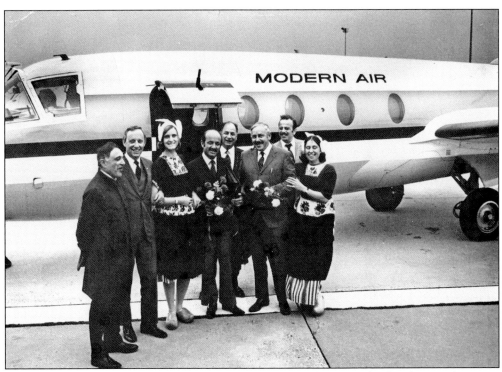

Gulf American had an extensive sales team spread out around New England and across the ocean in Europe. Teams worked in cities such as Hartford, Boston, Providence, Buffalo, and Syracuse to entice would-be homebuyers into visiting Cape Coral. Overseas, offices in England and Germany worked on turning the Cape into a foreign vacation spot. The photograph above shows a 1970 sales trip to Amsterdam.

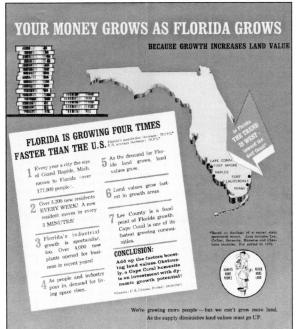

Besides selling the Florida dream, another sales technique was to tout what a good investment Cape Coral property would be. "Your Money Grows as Florida Grows" read one brochure. "If you had invested $1,000 in a Cape Coral home site in January 1958, you would be the owner of a choice home site that is valued at $3,560 today!"

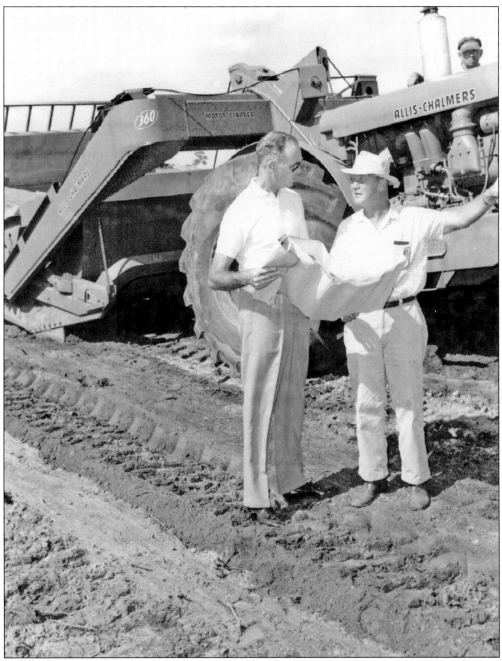

Connie Mack Jr. (left) was instrumental in the early development of Cape Coral. The son of famed Major League baseball player and manager Cornelius "Connie Mack" McGillicuddy, the junior Mack brought huge name recognition and instant credibility to the Rosen brothers' nascent city. According to historians, people were fascinated with the Mack family and knew about Cape Coral because they were here. Promotional materials at the time read as follows: "Connie Mack Jr. is the famous son of a famous father. Connie Mack, Sr., one of the pioneers of baseball, contributed much to its prestige and popularity. Connie, Jr. is doing the same for Cape Coral, and has helped to establish this rapidly growing community as one of America's outstanding new cities."

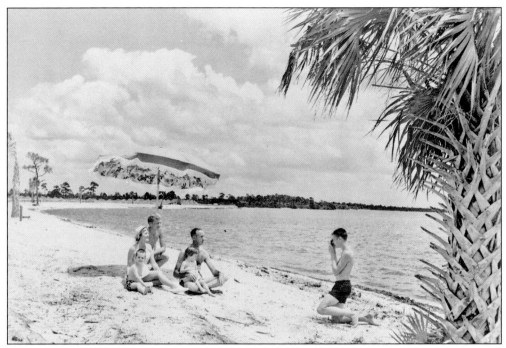

Connie Mack Jr. was on the Gulf American payroll and was involved in many aspects of Cape Coral's development. His image and images of him enjoying the good life with his family were used on many of the publicity materials that helped market Cape Coral to northerners. Despite this, the Mack family actually lived on the other side of the river from Cape Coral.

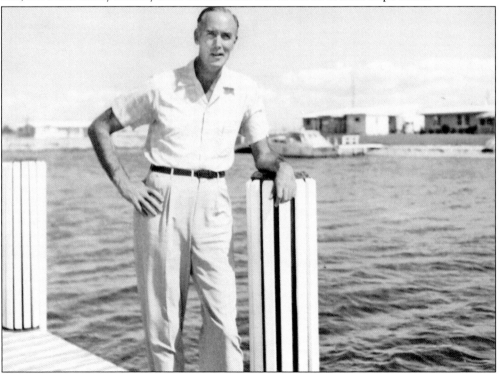

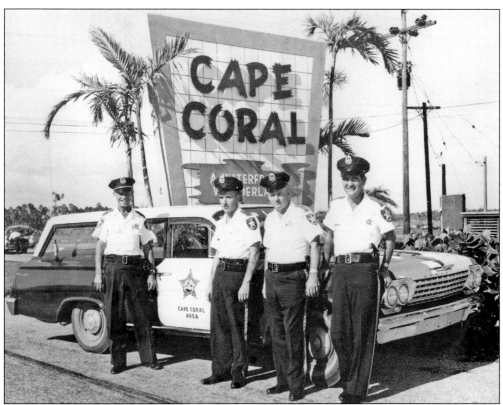

The first security force for Cape Coral was created in 1960 by Gulf American. The force consisted of Chief Earl Finerfrock and five officers. All were deputized by Lee County sheriff "Snag" Thompson. One security vehicle, a Chevrolet station wagon, served as a patrol car as well as an ambulance. It was equipped with a stretcher, oxygen, and tools for an emergency.

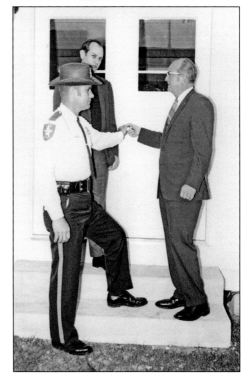

Eventually, Gulf American decided to get out of the security business and asked the Lee County sheriff to assign a deputy to Cape Coral. This lone officer was Val Everly, seen here in uniform facing Lee County sheriff "Snag" Thompson at the opening of the new Cape substation. Everly remembers spending much of his time keeping the community's teens out of harm's way. With little to do before the yacht club was built, some young people would get in trouble for underage drinking and causing minor problems. Currently Everly is retired and living in the Lehigh Acres area.

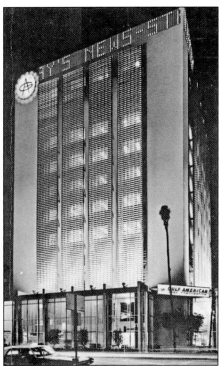

Corporate offices for Gulf American were located in Miami, eventually occupying a tall 11-story building at Seventy-ninth Street and Biscyane Boulevard. Leonard Rosen and Claude Kirk, who became Florida's governor in 1967, had a strained relationship. This, coupled with Kirk's crackdown on the developers who dominated the Florida Land Sales Board, led to increased oversight of Gulf American and similar ventures in the state. A 1967 *Wall Street Journal* article highlighting shady practices by Florida developers—including Gulf American—did not help.

In 1969, the Rosens, seen below with their wives, sold the company to GAC Corporation of Allentown, Pennsylvania. By that time, an incorporation drive to turn Cape Coral into a city had gained momentum. On August 11, 1970, the measure passed by a vote of 2,067 to 1,798, turning the Cape instantly into the second-largest city in the state. GAC continued to develop properties in Cape Coral for several years but declared bankruptcy in 1975. By then, the era of the Rosens was over.

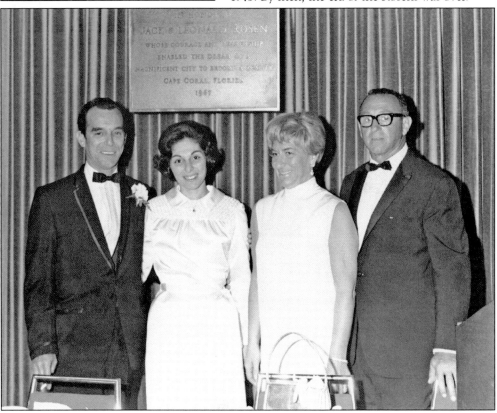

Three
AVIATION
CAPE CORAL FROM THE SKY

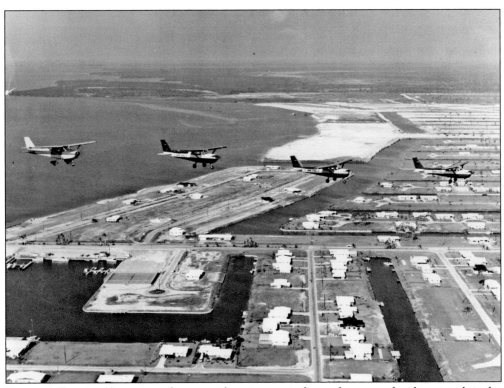

Despite selling itself as a waterfront paradise, it was airplanes that proved to be critical to the early success of the burgeoning community. To assist sales people marketing the Cape Coral dream, pilots in small planes took potential customers up into the wild blue yonder to give them an aerial view of their future property.

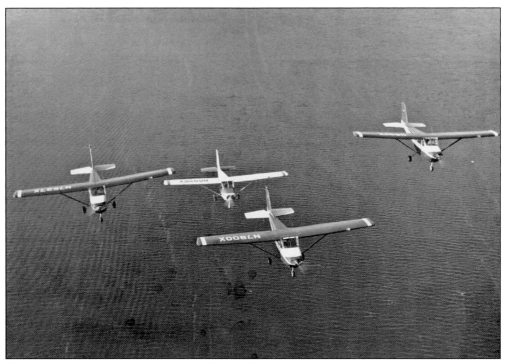

The statistics are impressive. At the peak of Gulf American's early sales, the company owned six planes and flew at least five flights an hour for at least six hours a day. Most of the planes were three-passenger, single-engine planes such as the workhorse Cessna 172. With this rate of activity, the company estimated that up to 500 potential buyers a day were viewing their development and Cape Coral from the air.

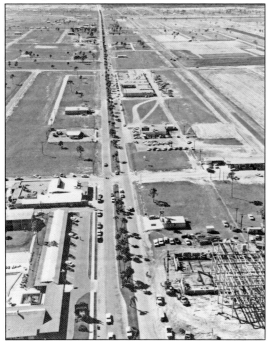

Originally, there was no formal airport. With Cape Coral Parkway divided by a median, planes took off and landed on the southernmost lane. As the community grew and traffic increased, security guards would stop cars at each end of the parkway to make way for planes loaded with eager passengers. At others times Coronado Parkway was used.

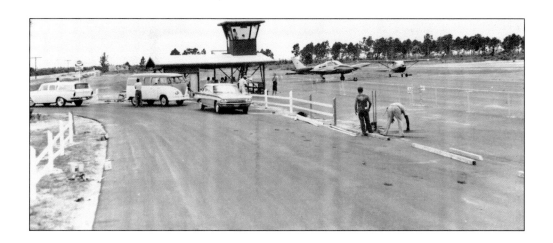

Later another roadway was used as an airstrip in Cape Coral—a stretch of Southeast Forty-seventh Terrace, just west of Del Prado Boulevard. Planes also landed right on the road there, so drivers had to beware. In 1962, the community saw the opening of the Cape Coral Airport. It was located on the west side of Del Prado Boulevard, south of Twenty-first Street near Everest Parkway. A 4,000-foot runway was available. Initially this facility was just for Gulf American planes and other local pilots. Eventually a few commercial flights would land at Cape Coral. In 1965, all Gulf American sales flights were transferred to Page Field in Fort Myers.

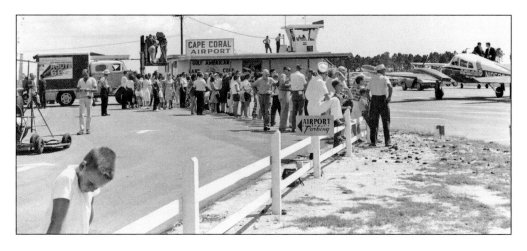

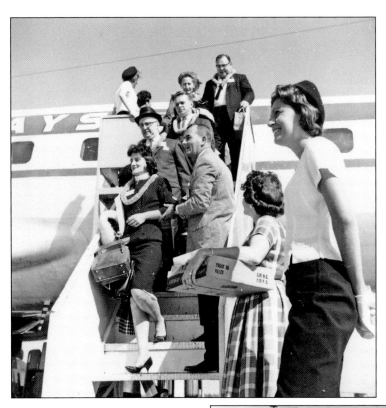

In the early 1960s, potential customers were flown in daily to Page Field near Fort Myers. From there, most passengers were bused to southern Cape Coral. However, VIPs were occasionally flown over to the Cape in Gulf American planes. Eventually Gulf American decided it was too expensive to keep contracting out these airline services, so they bought a company called Modern Air Transport and began charter flights between Cape Coral and many northern cities.

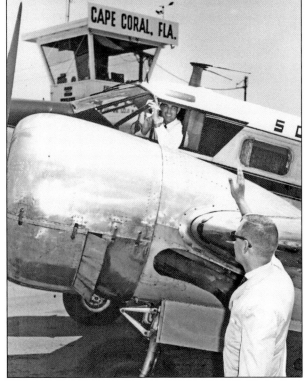

In this photograph, Bob Finkernagel, the managing director of Gulf American, is seen talking to a pilot with Southeast Airlines. In 1963, Southeast Airlines flew two flights a day carrying 10 passengers each in twin-engine Beechcraft planes from Miami to Cape Coral for $28 a ticket. This was unrelated to sales efforts and was purely air service between the two regions.

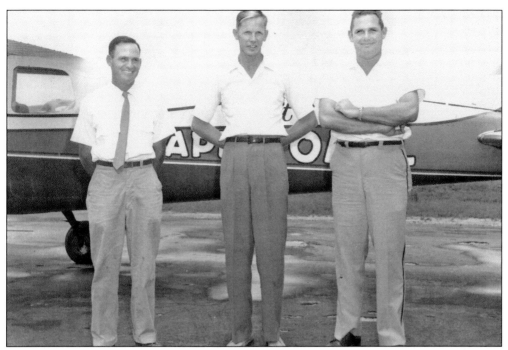

Pilots were crucial to the success of Cape Coral. Ed Wilson was the company's first pilot. The name of the pilot on the left is unknown, but pilot Pete Petrie stands in the middle and pilot Joe Gibson is on the right. Pete Petrie, a former crop duster pilot and Korean War vet, would later open his own real estate company and become a competitor of Gulf American, his former employer.

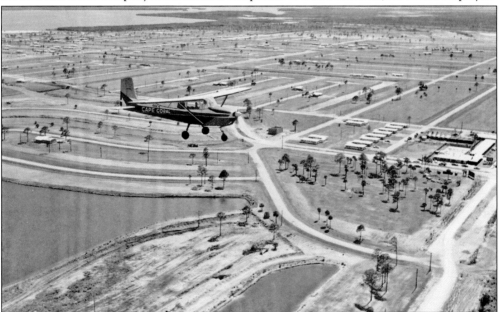

Most lots in the late 1950s were still inaccessible by automobile, so customers were flown over the area. Small bags of flour were dropped from the plane's window to mark their home site. The accuracy of these flour drops was suspect, as the pilots did not have many landmarks to go by. Nonetheless, sales continued to soar.

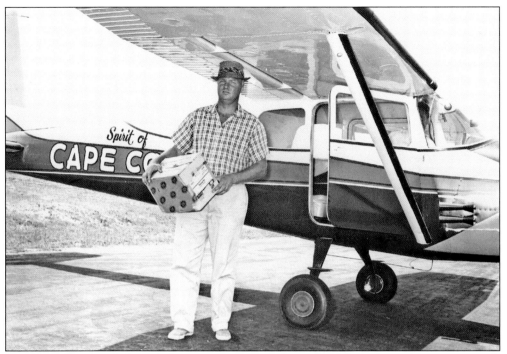

Pilot Joe Gibson regularly took clients on flights over Cape Coral. Despite a rule against animals on the small planes, one woman—a potential buyer—refused to go without her pet cat. Not wanting to lose a sale, Gibson's Gulf American bosses insisted the cat board with the customer. When the plane banked to return to the airport, it spooked the cat, which jumped onto Gibson's head and dug its claws into his scalp. Nonetheless, he safely landed the plane with the cat still clinging to his head. He vowed he would never take an animal on a flight again.

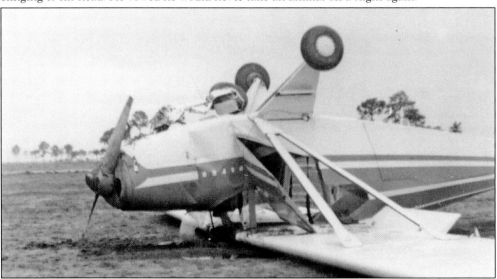

This intriguing photograph purports to show the Cape's first plane accident. Longtime resident Chris Schroder remembers seeing the plane on its roof. To his best recollection, it happened in the early 1960s. A plane was trying to land in a vacant lot near the Surfside Restaurant. As it came in, its wheels clipped some power lines, and the plane flipped. No one was seriously hurt.

Four
EARLY AMENITIES
Places to Go, Things to Do

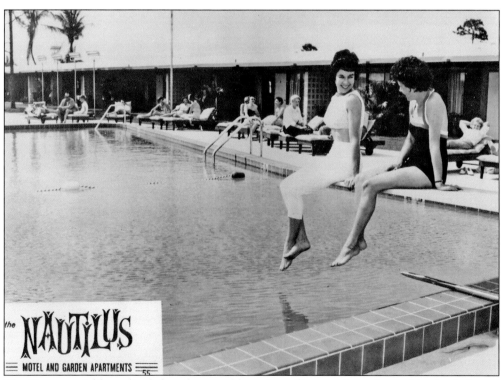

The Rosens quickly realized that they would need to offer a variety of amenities in their new community. These would be valuable both as diversions for the small but growing Cape Coral populace as well as attractive to potential customers looking at homes or land. This publicity photograph at the Nautilus Motel pool features Barbara Schwartz (left), wife of Gulf American manager Kenny Schwartz, and Doris Duffala (right), wife of local builder Butch Duffala.

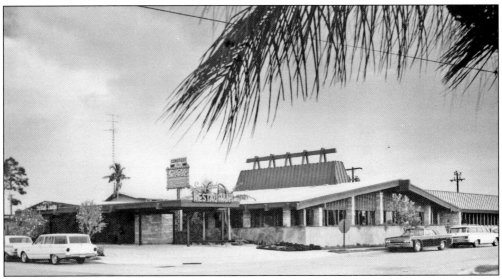

The corner of Del Prado Boulevard and Cape Coral Parkway was the site of the Cape's first business establishment. The Surfside Restaurant at the future Nautilus Motel complex opened for business in 1959 or early 1960, depending on the source. At the time, there were just 25 families or so calling the Cape home.

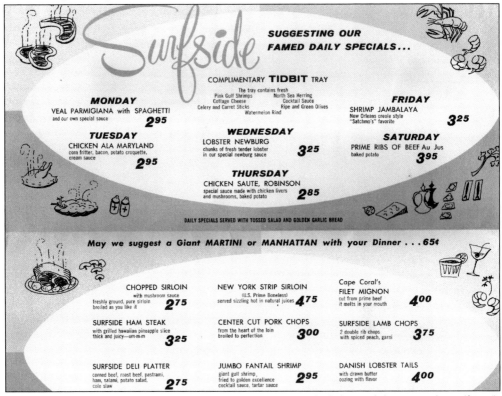

A 1960s-era menu from the Surfside Restaurant features such dishes as lobster Newburg ($3.25), jumbo fantail shrimp ($2.95), and chicken ala Maryland served with a corn fritter, bacon, potato croquette, and cream sauce ($2.95).

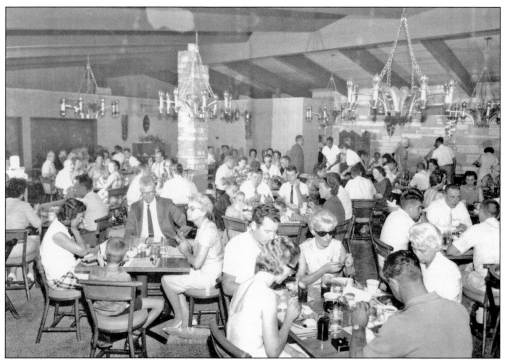

The complex included the Surfside Restaurant and coffee shop. It also featured a tiki lounge, parking lots, and a clubhouse, in addition to the motel. Its main function was as housing for Gulf American sales prospects, who were wined and dined at the Surfside. The Surfside also served as a combination community hall, general store, and post office for the early residents of Cape Coral.

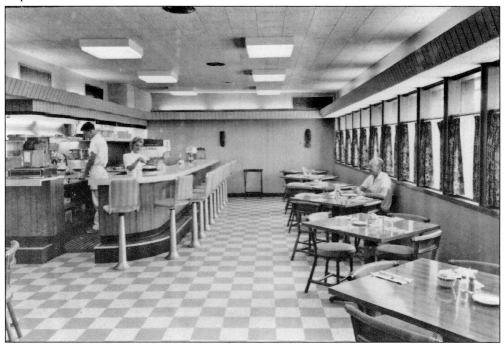

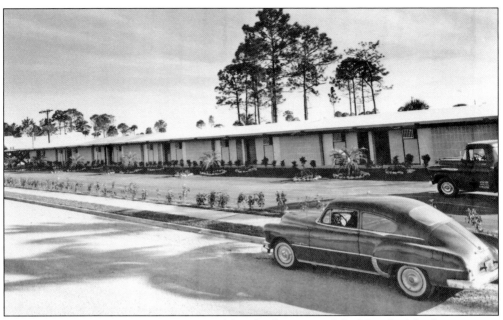

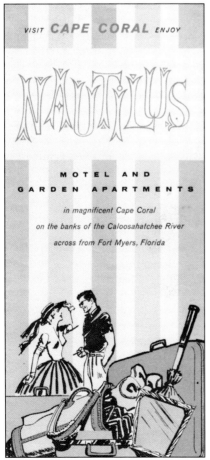

After the first units of the Nautilus Motel were completed, some community activities moved from the Surfside to the Nautilus clubhouse. The pool was used as a community swimming pool until the opening of the yacht and racquet club in 1962. The clubhouse was also used for community meetings and the nascent town's first church services. Early room rates at the Nautilus ran from $8 to $14.50 per night, depending on the room and the season.

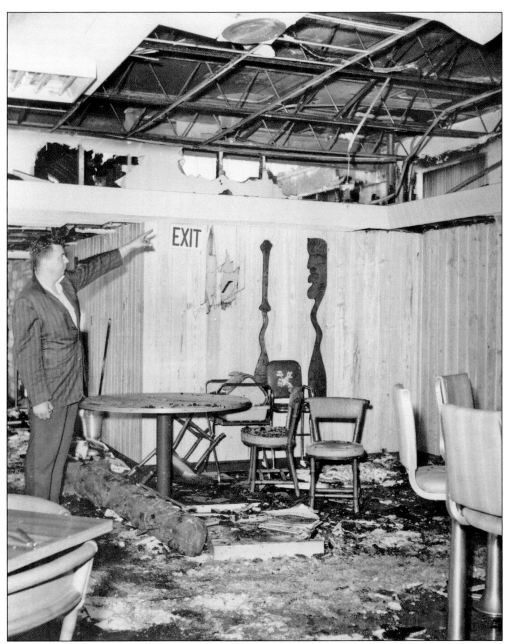

The Surfside Restaurant made news when a fire broke out inside the complex in the early 1960s. According to residents who remember the incident, a fire started in the kitchen and spread to the coffee shop. Fire crews were called from North Fort Myers, but they had a long drive ahead of them. At the time, Cape Coral only had a volunteer fire department. Aage Schroder Jr. was the assistant fire chief. He was given this position because he built swimming pools for a living and had a truck with a pump on it. When the Surfside caught on fire, Schroder and his fellow firefighters rushed to the site. They had to run hoses from the pump to a nearby canal and then to the scene of the fire. It was a time-consuming process. Nevertheless, the Surfside was saved, the damage was repaired, and the restaurant reopened.

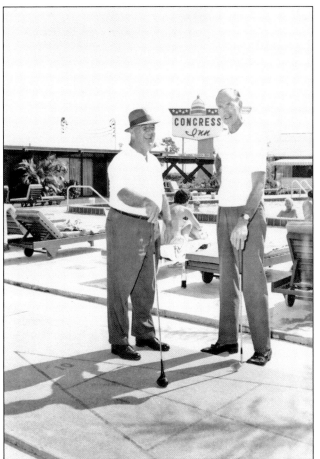

Gulf American undertook many ventures, and one of them was the purchase of the Congress Inn chain of motels. They changed the name of their Nautilus Motel to the Congress Inn. It later reverted back to the Nautilus Inn. In 1971, the complex was sold for a little more than $1 million. Both the Nautilus and the Surfside structures are long gone, but the Nautilus Motel sign was saved for a time and moved to Four Freedoms Park in the Cape. Unfortunately, it is no longer there. In the photograph at left, the taller of the two men standing by the pool is the well-known Connie Mack Jr. The other photograph is a postcard touting the motel's new name.

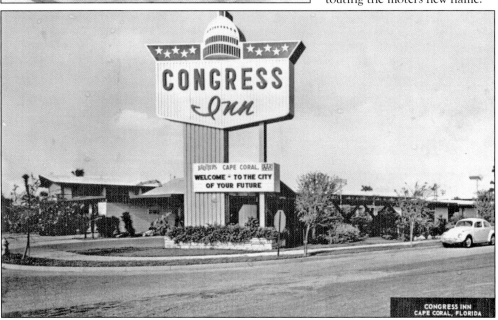

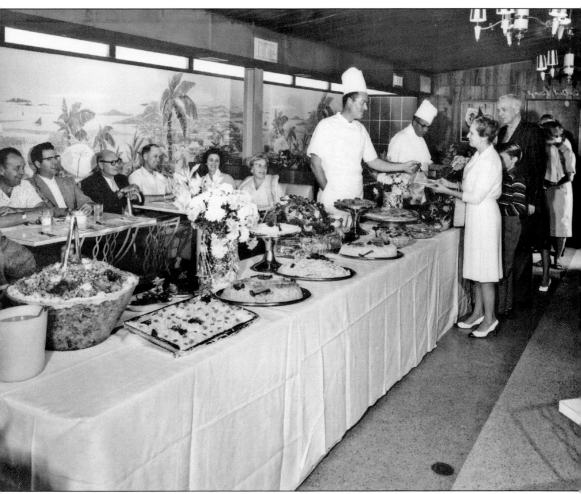

The land where the Surfside and Nautilus once sat is still a major center of activity in southern Cape Coral, standing at the very busy intersection of Cape Coral Parkway and Del Prado Boulevard. Currently the property is home to a Perkins restaurant. Believe it or not, a motel still stands there too. For years, it was part of the Quality Inn chain, and many might be surprised to know it was officially known as the Nautilus Quality Inn, even though that name did not appear on the sign. More recently, the property has become a Holiday Inn Express. The only part of the original complex still standing is the garden apartments located behind the Surfside and Nautilus. They were built at the same time as the long-gone structures and continue to serve as apartments today. One section is now a restaurant.

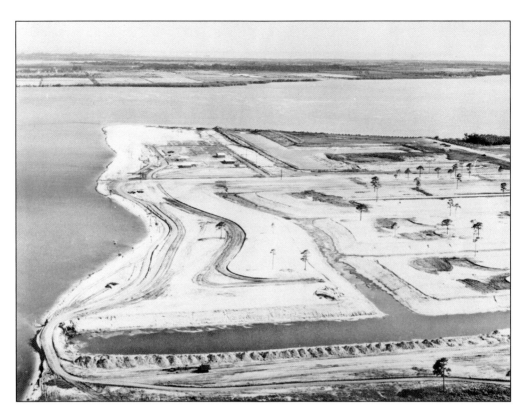

There were not many boats in Cape Coral in 1958, but any that were in town likely tied up often at this dock that would become the center of the future Cape Coral Yacht and Racquet Club, often just called the yacht basin. The larger boat in the picture below is the *Trident II*, the craft that Gulf American salesmen used to show prospective property buyers around the shores and canals of Cape Coral. Wally Pearson was the captain of the *Trident II* and also the harbormaster at the yacht basin. Longtime resident Chris Schroder recalls going fishing on the *Trident II*. He could not have been more than seven or eight years old at the time, and during one fishing expedition, he landed a sand shark. The fish was only about 3 feet long, but to a little boy, it was a memory to last a lifetime.

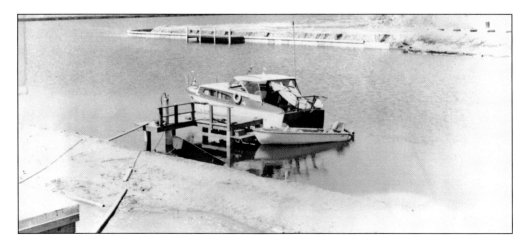

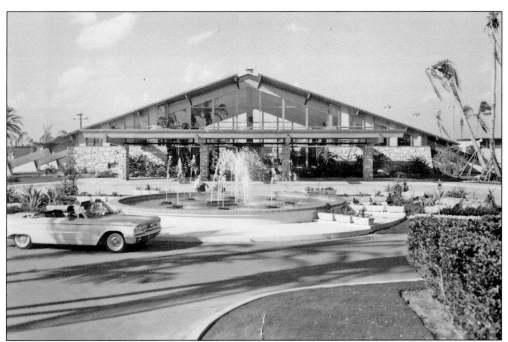

The Cape Coral Yacht and Racquet Club opened in June 1962. The Rosens had promised the amenity to the early families that settled in the Cape. Perhaps more importantly to the Rosens, it was yet another great amenity for their salesmen to tout while trying to close a land deal. This popular community recreation complex also included an Olympic-size swimming pool, tennis courts, shuffleboard, a 200-slip boat basin, and a sandy beach. It was free to all residents of Cape Coral. In 1963, Gulf American began hosting an intercollegiate tennis tournament on the yacht club's four courts. The company provided food and lodging as well as some wonderful trophies. The tournament's reputation grew, and more and more colleges came to the Cape to compete. Despite its success, the tournament was discontinued in 1970 after it was deemed too expensive.

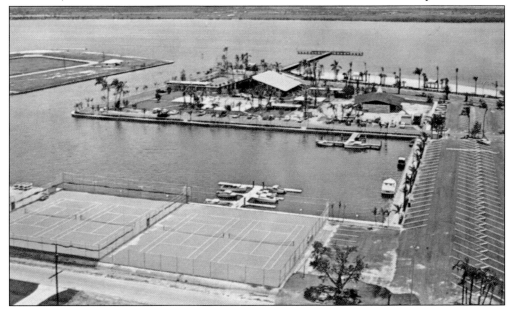

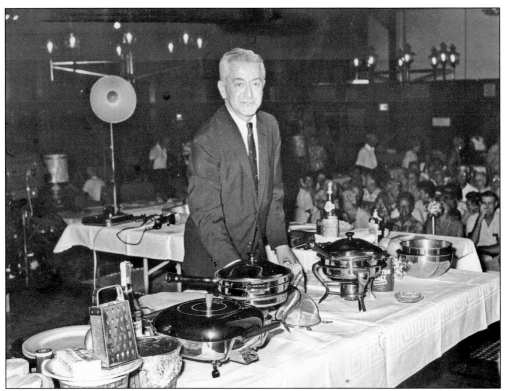

The club facility at the yacht club was a luxurious 10,000-square-foot building costing more than $750,000 to construct. The building contained a huge main lounge that could be converted into a meeting or banquet room with seating for 500. There was also a television and billiards, a reading room, a snack bar, and kitchen facilities. Much of the structure remains the same today.

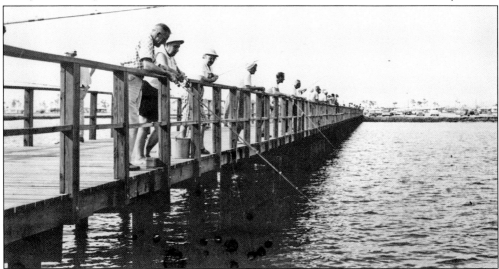

The fishing pier at the yacht club was built in 1960. It was 620 feet long with a 200-foot T at the end. Originally the structure had no lights, posing a hazard to watercraft at night. There was a tackle shop at the pier—the "Bait Shack," as many locals called it—where shrimp could be purchased before hitting the boards for a day of casting and catching the best the Gulf had to offer.

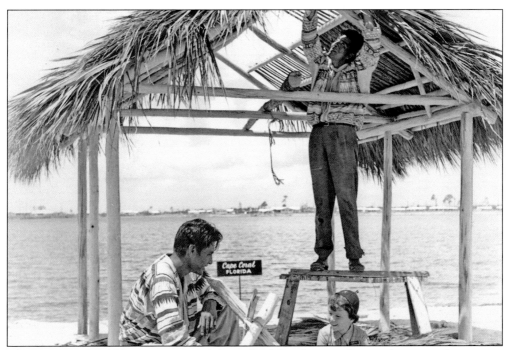

The Rosens and Gulf American wanted the yacht club to be something truly spectacular to prove that Cape Coral was going to be the paradise they had promised. They even went so far as to have true Native Americans from Florida's Seminole tribe come and build traditional chickee huts on the yacht club's beach. Residents and guests relaxing at the club used these thatched-roof structures as cabanas.

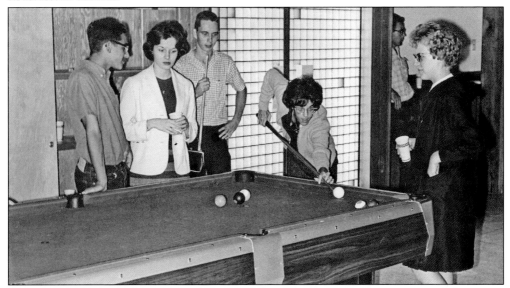

One of the buildings at the yacht and racquet club was a teen center. It was commonly known as the "Teen Club" or the "Key Club." It was designed for the exclusive use of the younger residents of Cape Coral, each of whom had his or her own key to the center's front door. The Teen Club opened in September 1962. Famous broadcaster Hugh Downs came to the opening, as did popular singer Anita Bryant.

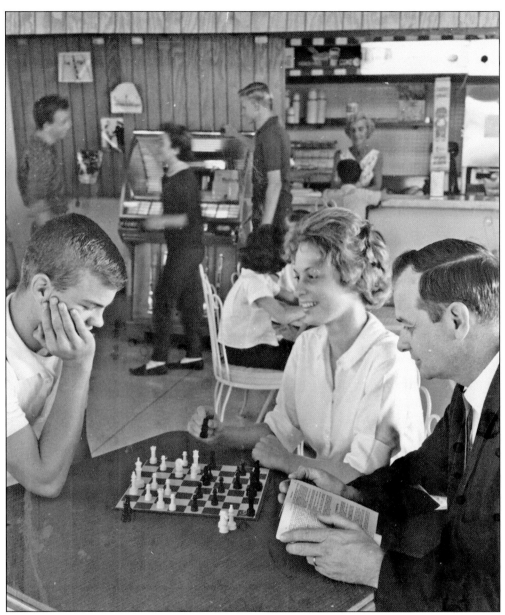
Cape Coral historian Paul Sanborn was the manager of the entire yacht club complex, which included the Teen Club. Paul is seen in this vintage photograph playing or watching a game of chess with his daughter, Carol, and a young man, Tom Brubaker. Sanborn recalls how proud having the Teen Club made the young people of Cape Coral and how serious they took this responsibility. On one occasion, one of the glass windowpanes that surrounded the building was broken. When Paul found out about it, he was angry and he ordered the custodian to clear out the Teen Club and lock it up. The young people were upset and went to complain to Paul. He said it would stay locked until they brought him the teen who broke the window. Within two hours, in trooped a group of kids with the guilty party. He got sent home with his parents, and the rest of the group was let back into the building.

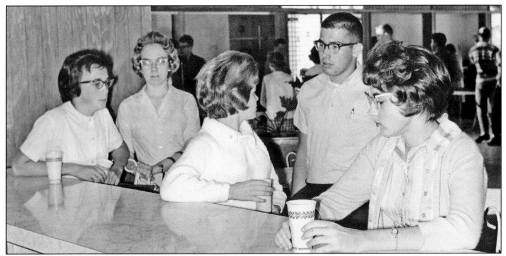

The Teen Club featured all the things that any 1960s teenager would have loved. There was an old-fashioned soda fountain, a jukebox, a pool table, and sofas and chairs for hanging out. Besides having their own keys to the Teen Club, there was a sign posted at the site that read, "No Adults Admitted Unless Accompanied by a Child." This was so unique that the nationwide *Teen Magazine* came to do a feature story on the club.

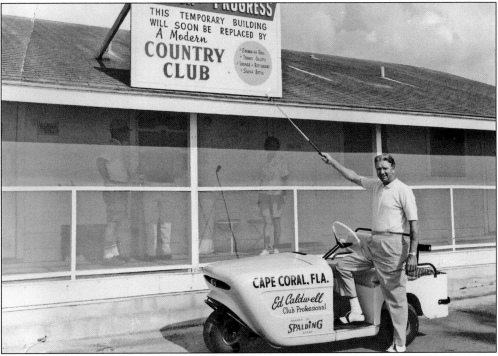

Gulf American continued its plan of offering the best amenities to lure new customers to Cape Coral by building the nine-hole Cape Coral Country Club golf course. Opening day was July 8, 1961. A second nine holes were added the following year. This photograph shows course professional Ed Caldwell in front of the pro shop and snack bar building. This building still exists, albeit in a different location. Today it is part of the Cape Coral Historical Museum, where much of this book was compiled.

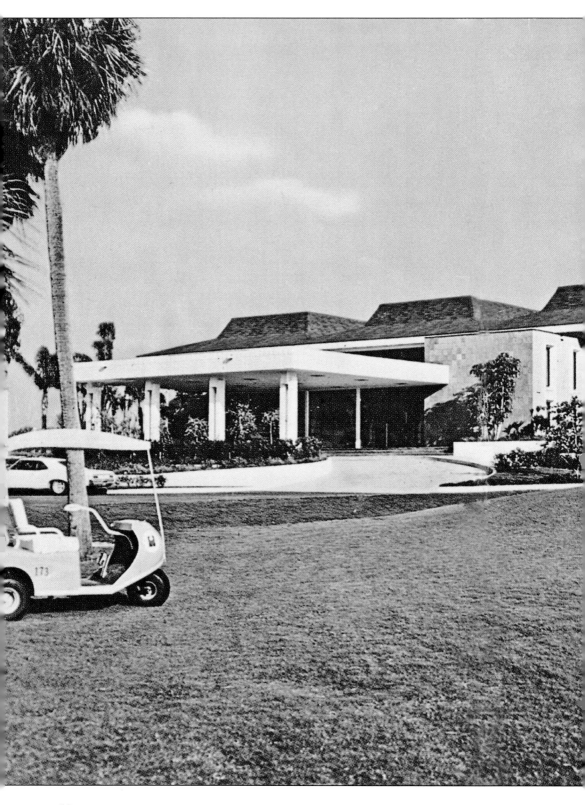

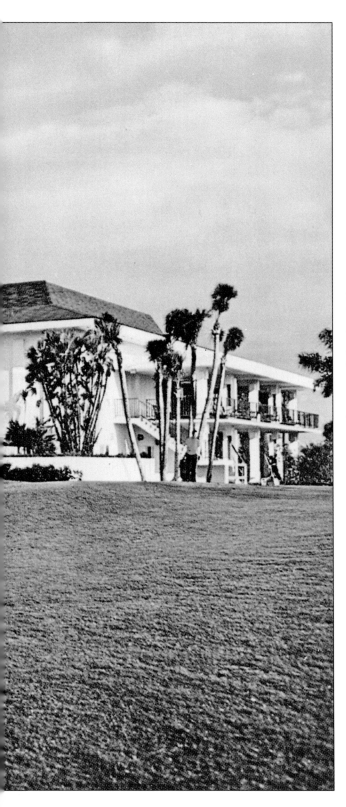

All along, a true country club had been promised, and in 1967, Gulf American kept that promise with the opening of the grand Cape Coral Country Club clubhouse. People who remember it say it was the most luxurious country club between Tampa and Miami. It featured the Royal Tee dining room, which was outfitted with rich, red leather furniture. There were banquet rooms with plush carpeting and fine, imported draperies. The club offered a concierge and valet parking. Downstairs, there was a coffee shop, a bar, a liquor store, and locker rooms. Initially some investors thought the Rosens were spending too much money on the club. The Rosens replied, "You people think this is a country club, but it's a sales tool." Even before the clubhouse was built, Gulf American constructed a 100-unit motel on the site known as the Cape Coral Country Club Inn, because the company was bringing in so many people on so many flights that the Nautilus Motel was regularly filling up. The inn was there for many years but eventually was sold, and the Banyan Trace condominiums were built in its place.

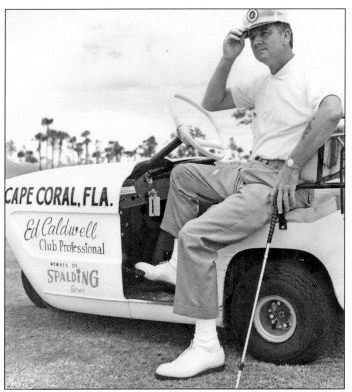

Ed Caldwell was the original golf pro at the Cape Coral Country Club. He arrived in May 1961 to help launch the new facility. A native of Macon, Georgia, Caldwell moved to the Rosens' new community with his wife and two young children, Eddie and Debra Lee. Previously, Caldwell had been the pro at the Dublin Country Club in Dublin, Georgia. Caldwell had won a number of pro-am tournaments during his career and was considered a great promoter of golf as well as a skilled player and instructor. As of this writing, he is retired and living in Homosassa Springs, Florida.

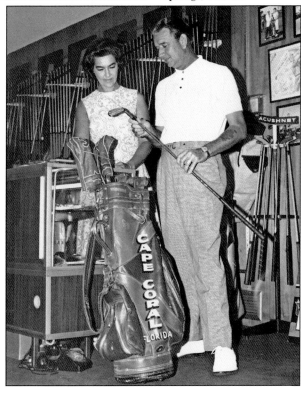

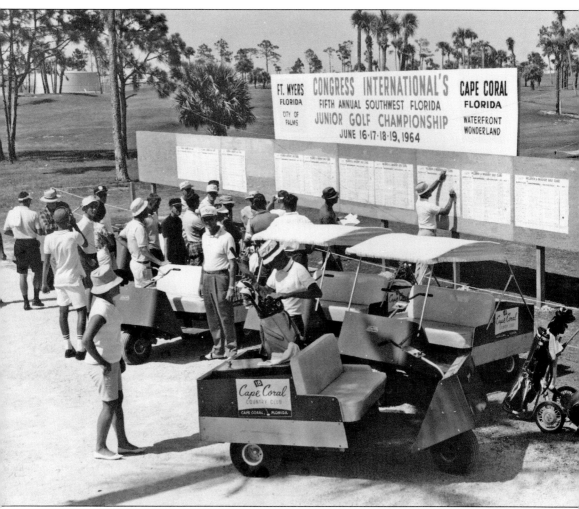

The Cape Coral Country Club started holding an intercollegiate golf tournament in 1963. This tournament grew steadily in size and reputation, to the point that in 1972, the club was given the honor of hosting the NCAA golf tournament. It was the first time the tournament had been played in the South, and the country club and tournament organizers spent more than a year preparing. Everything was set until a hurricane blew through the area the weekend before the tournament. Flights were canceled, which delayed the arrival of many teams. The torrential rains soaked the course and prevented early practice rounds. Nonetheless, the skies cleared by Monday, practices took place Tuesday, and the tournament started on schedule on Wednesday. The tournament ended with history being made. With no provision for a playoff, University of Texas teammates Tom Kite and Ben Crenshaw were both declared winners. Both golfers went on to great success on the PGA Tour. The annual intercollegiate tournament was last held in 1978.

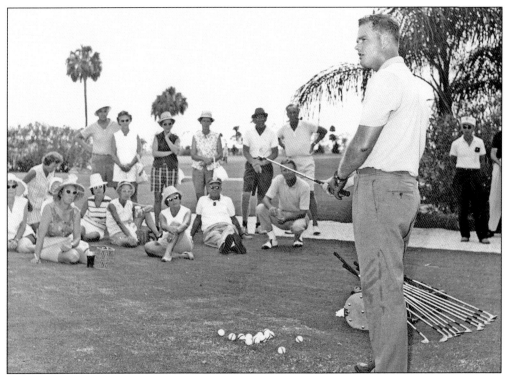

The main hazard on the country club's golf course was the occasional alligator. Other than occasionally having to pull a golf cart out of the water, life at the club was calm. The main excitement came when Gulf American would bring a celebrity or dignitary to town. Most were wined and dined at the country club, and many played a round of golf while there.

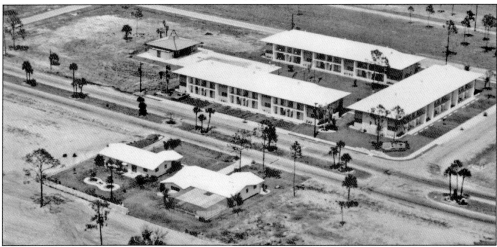

The Country Club Estates Apartments on Palm Tree Boulevard were some of the first apartments built by Gulf American in Cape Coral. They were located near the golf course. While these apartments preceded today's modern condominium concept, they nevertheless served the same purpose as second homes for retirees who wanted to spend time in Florida and live on a golf course but did not need a single-family home. Today the area is still known as Country Club Estates, and the apartment complex is still there.

Five

Rose Garden
The Famous Cape Coral Gardens

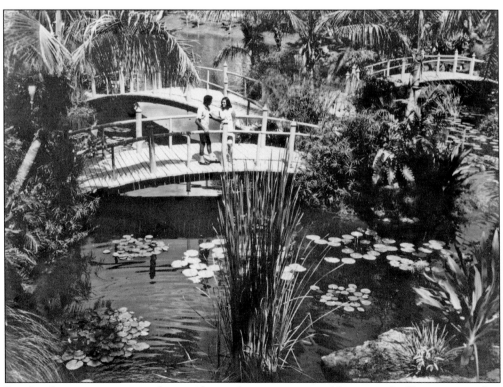

Besides the many amenities that residents of a new town would expect, the Rosens wanted to give Cape Coral something truly spectacular, something that would become famous around the country and lure visitors and potential customers. Their answer was the famous Cape Coral Gardens, more commonly known locally as the Rose Garden. This publicity photograph is from the beautiful Aloha Lagoon area.

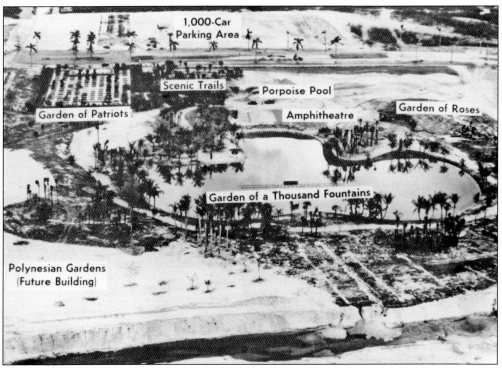

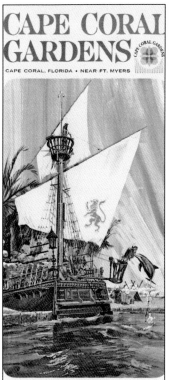

This fascinating photograph shows early construction underway on the Cape Coral Gardens. The finished version of the gardens was very similar to the original plan, although some names ended up undergoing a change. The Garden of a Thousand Fountains was the feature that became famous as the Waltzing Waters.

The Cape Coral Gardens opened in 1964, and an early brochure lays out the many attractions for visitors. These included the Porpoise Show, the Patriots Pavilion, the Garden of Patriots, the Aloha Lagoon, the Hanging Gardens, the Garden of Roses, and the famous Waltzing Waters.

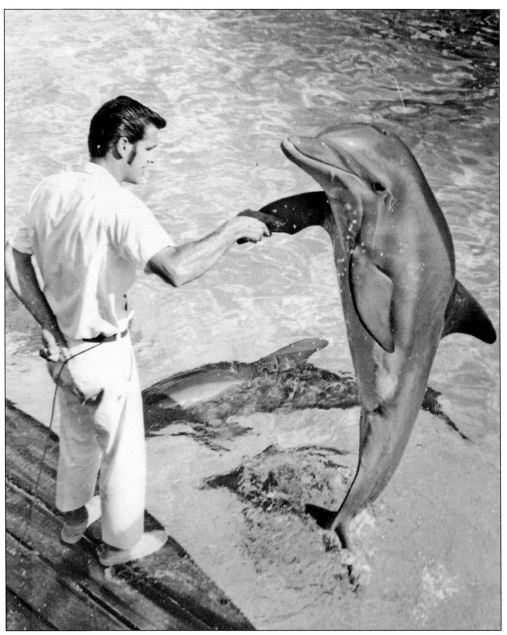

Jack Scarpuzzi, seen here, was the porpoise trainer for many years at the Cape Coral Gardens. The enclosure was a 110-foot pool holding more than 200,000 gallons of salt water. Usually the gardens had four porpoises at a time that would perform in up to four shows a day. The porpoise show revolved around a faux Spanish galleon next to the pool where trainers would put the animals through their paces. On command, the porpoises could leap up to 16 feet out of the pool and take a fish held in Scarpuzzi's teeth. The first time he performed this trick, Bubbles the star porpoise split Scarpuzzi's lip. In a moving tale from the gardens, Scarpuzzi has told of the time his two-year-old child was at other end of pool and suddenly fell in. Scarpuzzi began running around the pool, but one of the porpoises scooped up the child and held it up with its nose until he could rescue the youngster. Scarpuzzi went on to work at Marineland of Florida near St. Augustine.

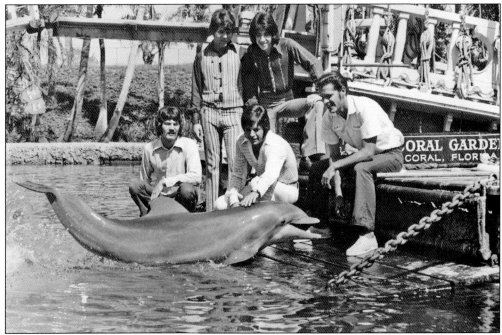

Aage Schroder III recalls working at the gardens. One of his jobs was putting on an old-fashioned diving suit—weighted boots and a big helmet—and cleaning the pool with an underwater vacuum. Often, one of the porpoises would jump out of its pen, swim across the pool, and unplug the vacuum hose. The teen would have to clamber back across the pool to plug it back in, only to have the mammal repeat its prank over and over.

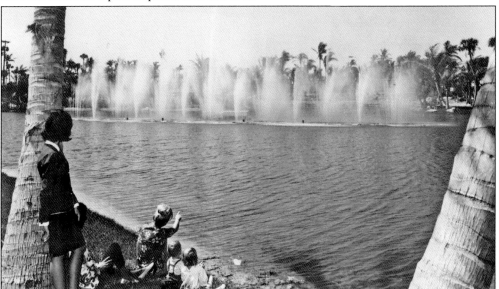

The Waltzing Waters were perhaps the most famous attraction at the Cape Coral Gardens. These dancing jets of water changed color and swayed in sync with music in an amazing show. Otto Przystawik of Germany designed the fountains. In 1920s Berlin, he operated Przystawik's Dancing Fountains. The Rosens hired him to develop a much larger, more lavish display for their gardens. Otto's son, Gunther Przystawik, operated the Waltzing Waters fountains in Cape Coral.

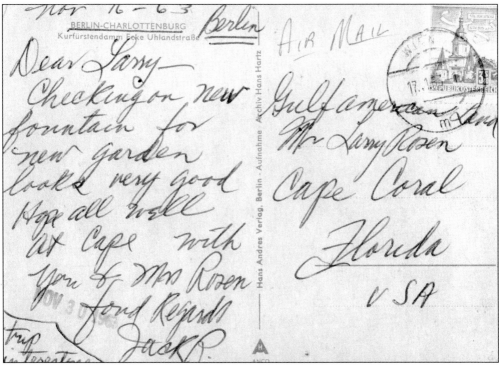

This historic postcard from Jack Rosen was sent while on a trip to Europe. He was there to examine the new Waltzing Waters fountains he had commissioned for his Cape Coral Gardens. It reads in part, "Checking on new fountain for garden. Looks very good." Little did he know how good—the Waltzing Waters in Cape Coral became famous across America.

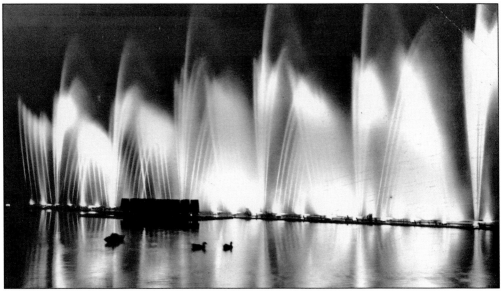

The fountain array was 137 feet long and contained more than 800 water jets that shot a spray 85 feet high. Some 3,500 feet of piping was required to operate the fountains, and the resulting combination of flowing water, shimmering hues, and magical music captivated audiences. From a natural amphitheater on a hill rising above the fountain lake, visitors witnessed a spectacular show.

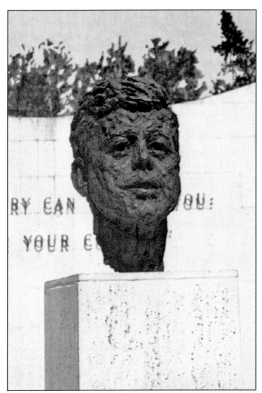

The Cape Coral Gardens featured a famous, somber Garden of Patriots. Among its features were busts of many historic patriotic Americans. Renowned sculptor Robert Berks crafted the bust of Pres. John F. Kennedy, whose assassination was still fresh in the minds of millions. It was 17 inches high and sat on a free-form white concrete cupola overlooking a reflecting pool. Quotes from Kennedy appeared on a wall behind the pool. Other patriots featured in the garden included Presidents Harry Truman, Thomas Jefferson, Dwight Eisenhower, and Abraham Lincoln. There were also busts of entertainer Bob Hope, opera singer Marian Anderson, and Sen. Everett Dirksen. Many of these busts were lost when the gardens closed, but some of them were safeguarded and today reside at the Cape Coral Historical Museum.

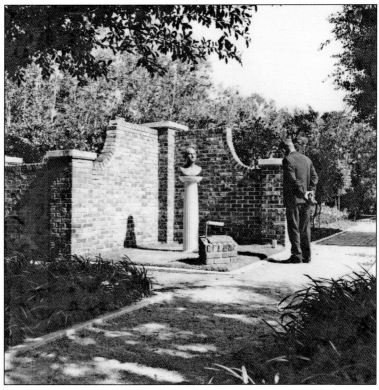

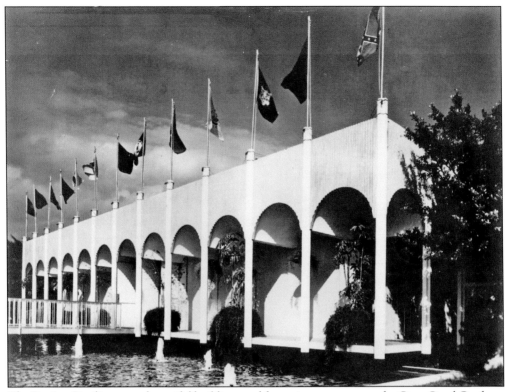

The Patriots Pavilion was a beautiful building used for various purposes at the Cape Coral Gardens. In one respect, it was a grand entrance to the Garden of Patriots statuary garden. It also contained space for an ever-changing variety of historical, artistic, and other exhibits. Finally, it was the location of administrative offices and the requisite Cape Coral Gardens gift shop.

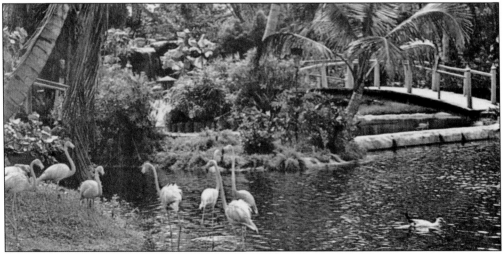

Aloha Lagoon was just what the name suggests—lush, subtropical foliage bordering tree-rimmed lakes, trees and flowers everywhere, and some man-made waterfalls to boot. Flaming torches, jungle birds—including lots of flamingos—native tiki idols, and high-arched Polynesian-style bridges completed the Pacific theme. During its heyday, many television commercials were filmed in the Aloha Lagoon.

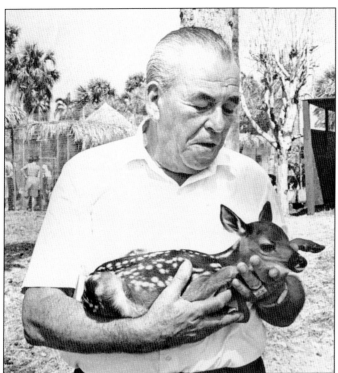

A complete zoo with the usual menagerie of elephants, lions, tigers, alligators, monkeys, and macaws was yet another component of the Cape Coral Gardens. Larry Rosen, seen in these photographs with various denizens of the zoo, was the director of the gardens. Longtime residents recall that the flamingos in the zoo were kept pink through the combination of a special food and dye. The fanciful birds' wings were clipped, but at least one of them was known for running away. The Pearson boys, who worked at the zoo, would have to hop in a boat to chase it and spend hours wading around trying to recapture the wayward bird.

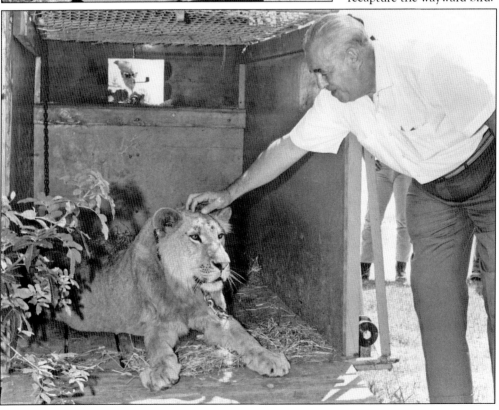

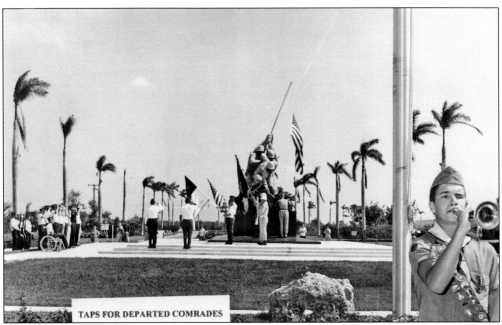

TAPS FOR DEPARTED COMRADES

Standing near the entrance to the Garden of Patriots was a replica of the famous U.S. Marine Corps War Memorial, depicting marines raising the American flag on Mount Suribachi. The original was created by Felix de Weldon and stands next to Arlington National Cemetery. De Weldon himself cast the Cape Coral version in stone to a one-third scale. Surrounding it were five flagpoles bearing the banners of the United States, England, France, Spain, and the Confederacy, representing the various nations that had ruled over Florida. The Cape Coral Gardens closed in 1970. The land sat abandoned for many years, and the Iwo Jima statue was vandalized. In 1981, the original sculptor returned and refurbished the monument. It was moved to a bank on Del Prado Boulevard, where it stayed for many years. In the mid-1990s, it was moved again to its current location, sitting proudly near the busy Veterans Parkway and Midpoint Bridge.

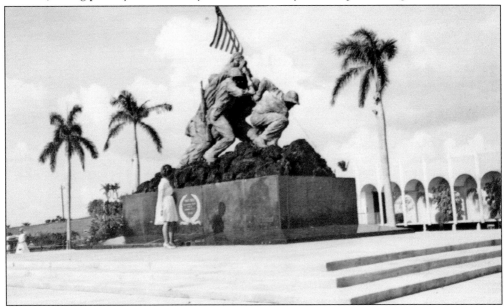

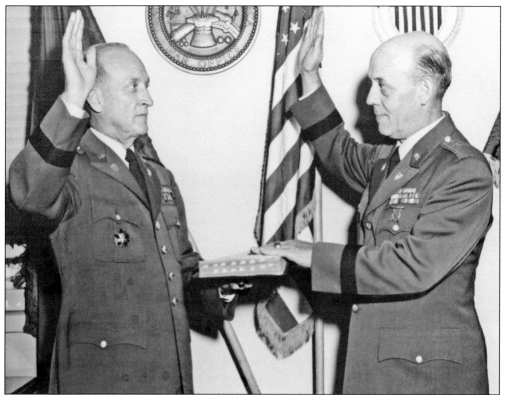

Retired Maj. Gen. Bruce Easley (right) had a unique role in the history of Cape Coral. He was the official liaison between Gulf American and the U.S. military. It was his job to promote Cape Coral as a retirement spot for veterans leaving the service. It certainly worked, because Cape Coral went on to have one of the highest concentrations of veterans of any community in the country, which is true to this day. Easley was actively involved in the Garden of Patriots and other military memorials at the Cape Coral Gardens.

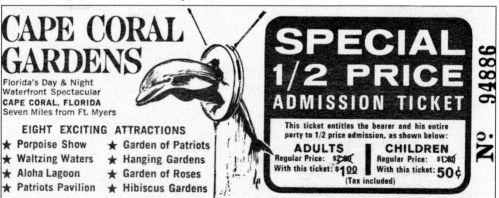

The Porpoise Show and a few other attractions were moved to the German-American Club and operated under the name "Aquaramax" for several years. The Waltzing Waters can be seen today at the Shell Factory in North Fort Myers. When Gulf American was sold, the new owners felt they could not keep the expensive attraction open. The much beloved but unprofitable Cape Coral Gardens closed in 1970. Today the Tarpon Point Marina development sits on land that was once the Cape Coral Gardens.

Six

CELEBRITIES
HOLLYWOOD GLAMOUR ON THE CAPE

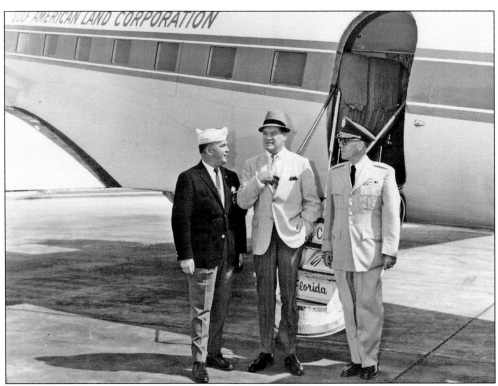

Just as they had used celebrities to sell their hair care products in the 1950s, the Rosens used Hollywood glamour to make Cape Coral seem like the hippest place in the country. Chief among the long list of top stars who made their way to Cape Coral over the years was the famous funny man Bob Hope.

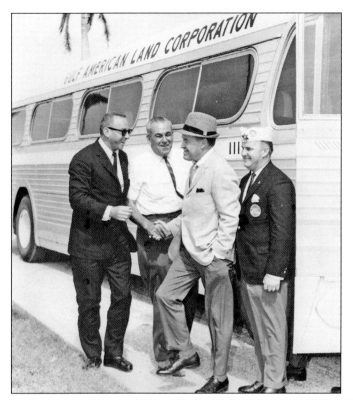

Bob Hope visited Cape Coral in 1966. He flew into Page Field in Fort Myers and took a bus to Cape Coral. He came to accept the local AMVET chapter's Patriot of the Year award for his long service to military men via the USO. Locals declared it "Bob Hope Day," and during his visit, he helped dedicate the Garden of Patriots and the AMVETS carillon organ at the Cape Coral Gardens. Some 5,000 people from across Southwest Florida turned out to see Hope that day.

The visit was great public relations for Gulf American. Cape Coral historian Paul Sanborn, then community relations director with the company, drove Hope to the stage at the gardens. Sanborn recalls that he pulled up with the driver's side closest to the stage. Hope looked at the crush of fans and said, "You're not going to let me out in that mess." Sanborn dutifully repositioned the car so Hope could get closer to the steps of the stage without being accosted.

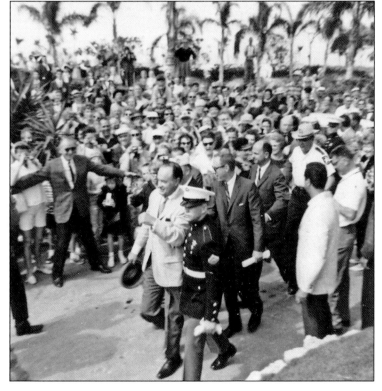

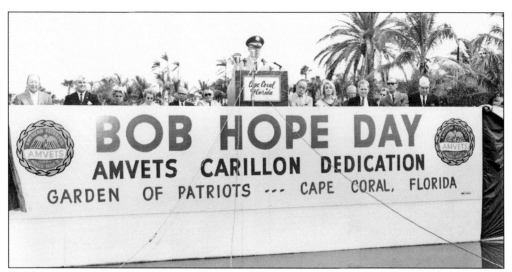

On that first visit, Bob Hope was in Cape Coral for less than a day—actually just a few hours. He returned to Southwest Florida on several other occasions, including a 1973 golf tournament on Marco Island and a 1979 sold-out concert before 8,000 people at the Lee County Arena (today the Lee Civic Center). However, as far as anyone knows, he never again returned to Cape Coral.

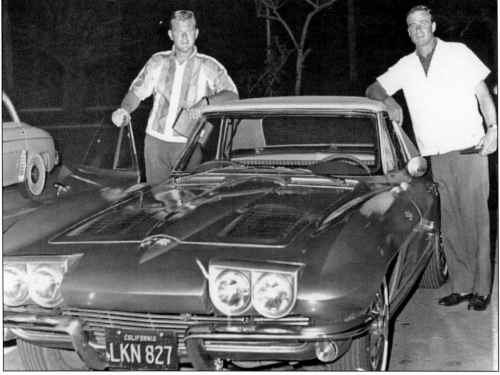

In 1963, one of the biggest things to ever happen in Cape Coral occurred. Crews from the popular television show *Route 66* came to town to film scenes for several episodes. The show was about two young men who travel the country in their Corvette and have all sorts of encounters and adventures. In its fourth season, when it came to the Cape, the stars were Glenn Corbett and Martin Milner.

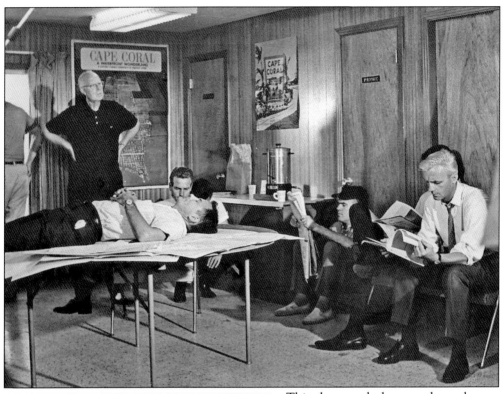

This photograph shows a rehearsal for *Route 66* taking place in the Surfside Restaurant. According to the International Movie Database, all or parts of three episodes were shot in Cape Coral. They were "Two Strangers and an Old Enemy," "Shadows of an Afternoon," and "Who Will Cheer My Bonnie Bride."

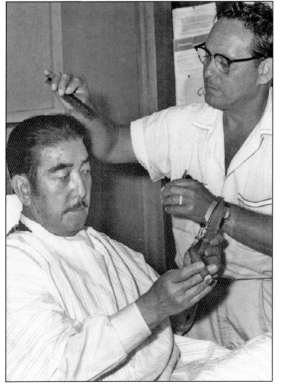

"Two Strangers and an Old Enemy" featured guest star Sessue Hayakawa, a famous Japanese actor who became a major star in early Hollywood. He was nominated for an Academy Award for Best Supporting Actor for the 1957 movie *The Bridge on the River Kwai*. Other actors listed as appearing in the Cape Coral episodes include Rip Torn and a young Gene Hackman.

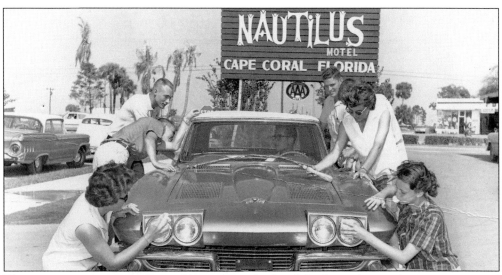

The young men starring in *Route 66* were heartthrobs of the day and created quite a stir around town. Cape native Pat Molter Emerson recalls how she and a friend, both 13 at the time, spent two weeks chasing Martin Milner and Glenn Corbett around town. However, security guards kept them from getting close to the filming locations. Finally the teens staked out the Nautilus Motel, where the stars were staying. Sure enough, they found them and got their picture taken with the celebrity duo.

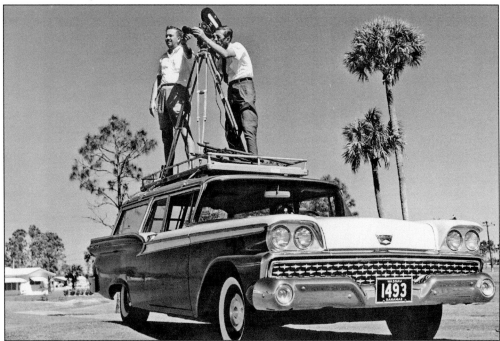

Cape Coral resident Chris Schroder recalls watching the show's actors film a bar fight scene at the Nautilus. They had a fake table that collapsed at the slightest touch and then would pop back up so they could film the scene over and over. Schroder also recalls a scene where Martin Milner was lying on a stretcher near a canal. A large mullet jumped in the water, startling the actor and causing him to leap up off the stretcher.

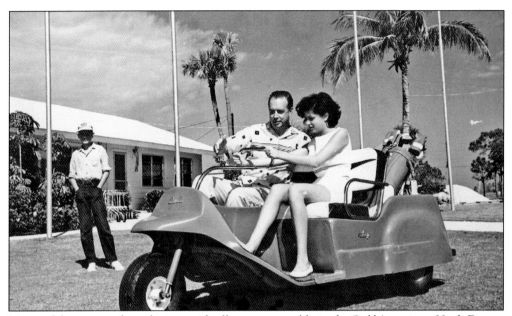

Many celebrities were brought in specifically to garner publicity for Gulf American. Hugh Downs was a well-known television announcer and personality in the 1950s. He was the announcer for *The Tonight Show* with host Jack Paar from 1957 to 1962. The Rosens brought Downs and his family to Cape Coral, where Downs spent time golfing at the Cape Coral Country Club.

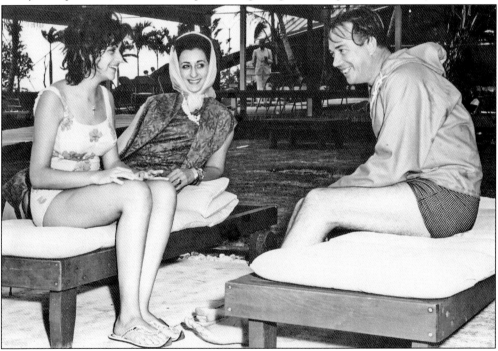

This photograph shows Downs and his family at the Teen Club at the Cape Coral Yacht and Racquet Club. While the family was in town, they stayed at the Nautilus Motel. During this same time period, Downs was the host of the television game show *Concentration*. Interestingly, winners on the show frequently won a home in Cape Coral as their grand prize.

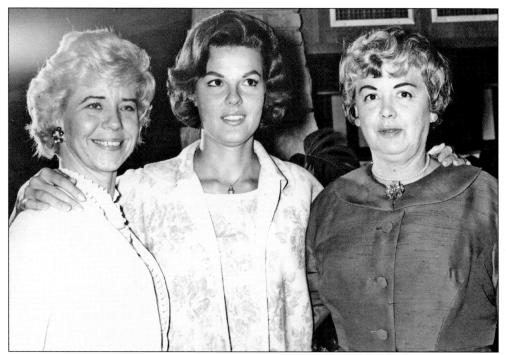

Anita Bryant was another big name who spent time in Cape Coral. Bryant was singer who released such songs as "Paper Roses" and "In My Little Corner of the World." Bryant came to Cape Coral at the invitation of the Rosen brothers. Her visit garnered positive publicity for their development and land sales business. The woman to her right is Eileen Bernard, personal secretary to the Rosens. Peggy Tanfield is on the left.

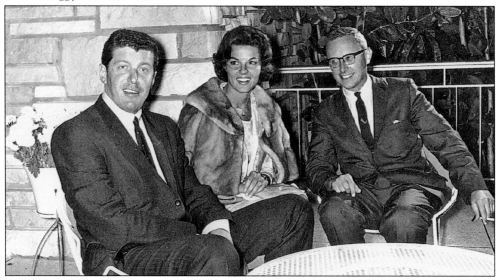

Singer Anita Bryant is seen with Gulf American managing director Bob Finkernagel (right) and an unidentified man. Bryant's ties with Florida would grow in the late 1960s, when she became a spokeswoman for the Florida Citrus Commission. In that role, she sang the ditty "Come to the Florida Sunshine Tree" and was seen in commercials saying, "Breakfast without orange juice is like a day with sunshine."

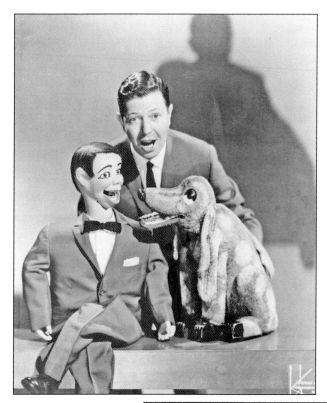

One of Cape Coral's most famous residents is Jimmy Nelson, who moved there in the mid-1960s. He was a nationally known ventriloquist who entertained children in the 1950s and 1960s in a series of Nestle chocolate commercials that ran on Saturday mornings. He was aided by his partners Danny O'Day and Farfel the Dog. As of this writing, Nelson still lives in Cape Coral.

Jimmy Nelson had a home in Cape Coral at the time with his wife, Betty Nelson, and their six children. Besides the Nestle commercials, he appeared at nightclubs and large fairs and did publicity for Chevrolet. The Nelsons reportedly did not have a television in their home because Jimmy spent so much time around the entertainment industry that he wanted to enjoy a break from it at home. This 1966 photograph was taken at the Cape Coral Gardens.

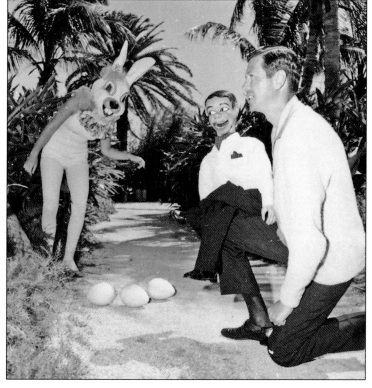

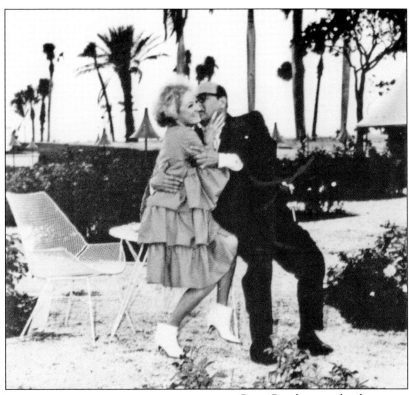

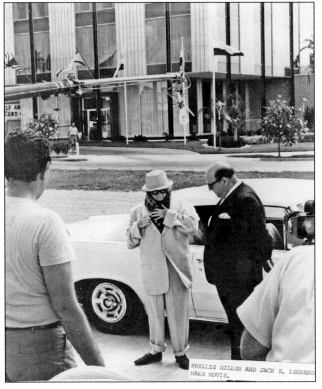

PHYLLIS DILLER AND JACK E. LEONARD MAKE MOVIE.

Cape Coral can make the unfortunate claim of being the location for one of the worst Hollywood films ever made. It was called *The Fat Spy* and came out in 1966. It was shot almost entirely in and around the Cape, including the Cape Coral Gardens. The movie starred Phyllis Diller and Jack E. Leonard as well as Jayne Mansfield and Brian Dunlevy. *The Fat Spy* was a musical comedy about various people invading an island off the Florida coast in search of the Fountain of Youth. The movie was so bad that it was only released in a few theaters before disappearing for decades. In 2004, a documentary named *The Fat Spy* one of the "50 Worst Movies Ever Made." Copies of the movie began appearing on DVD in the 1990s, often for sale at bargain and discount stores.

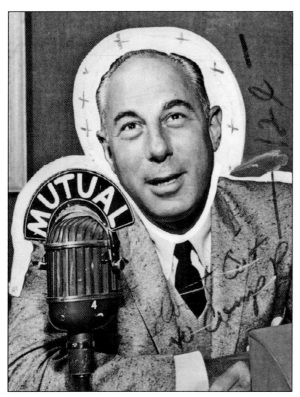

Bill Stern was a famous sportscaster. Among his claims to fame, he announced the nation's first remote sports broadcast and the first telecast of a Major League baseball game. Gulf American brought Stern to Cape Coral for publicity, hoping that he would make mention of the delightful new town while on the air, garnering the attention of his radio and television audiences. Bill Stern, seen in the photograph below with Connie Mack Jr., came to Cape Coral often in the 1960s. He bought a home site here, like so many other visitors to the community.

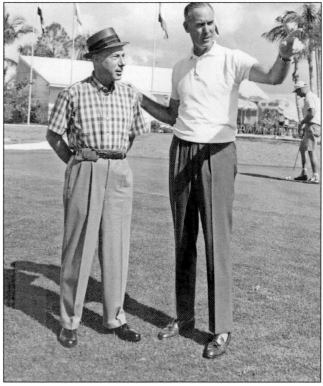

In the late 1960s, America was good friends with Ferdinand Marcos, the president of the Philippines. Never ones to pass up an opportunity for public relations, Gulf American managers invited Marcos's mother to visit Cape Coral. Historians say Josefa Edralin ended up purchasing some $200,000 worth of land in the community. In this photograph, Marcos's mother accepts a plaque in the Garden of Patriots

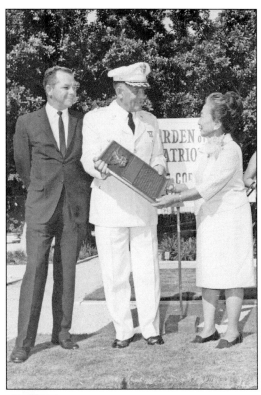

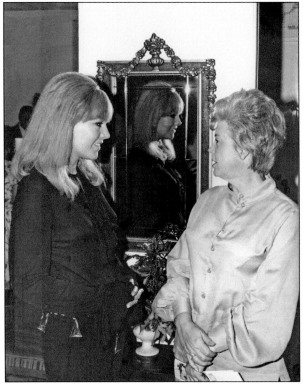

Actress Kim Novak is one of the rare Hollywood celebrities who did not come to Cape Coral on a public relations junket. Instead, she came to visit her parents, who lived on Palm Tree Boulevard near the country club. The elder Novaks lived in Gulf American's Serenade model home. Novak, who rose to great fame in the 1950s and starred in Alfred Hitchcock's hit movie *Vertigo*, reportedly garnered little attention when she visited. Locals recall seeing her attending mass at St. Andrew's Church.

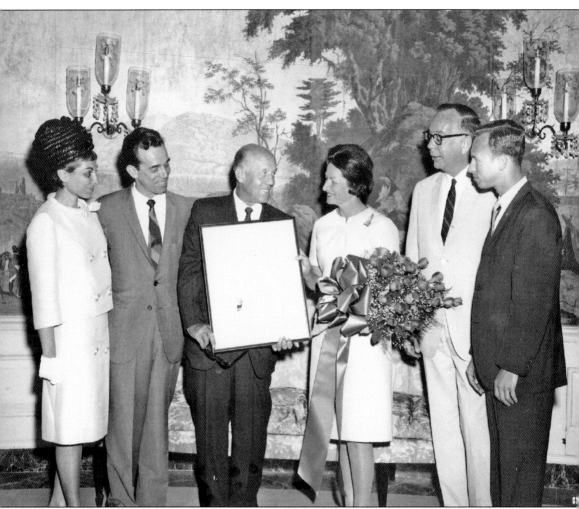

In this photograph from 1965, Lady Bird Johnson, the wife of Pres. Lyndon B. Johnson, accepts a dozen Cape Coral roses from representatives of the Garden of Patriots in Cape Coral. The group includes Jack Rosen and Gen. Bruce Easley (Ret.). The Cape Coral rose was a special hybrid rose created for the community as publicity for the Cape Coral Gardens. The gardens were planted with more than 40,000 rose bushes. Originally the Rosens planned to plant Cape Coral roses in every state capital across the nation. Some cities got their roses, but Gulf American never achieved its goal of all 50 states. Lady Bird Johnson was a lover of roses and willfully gave her support to the Gulf American rose planting program. The first rose bush of the program was planted at the White House in Washington, D.C.

Seven
Waterfront Wonderland
Life on the Water

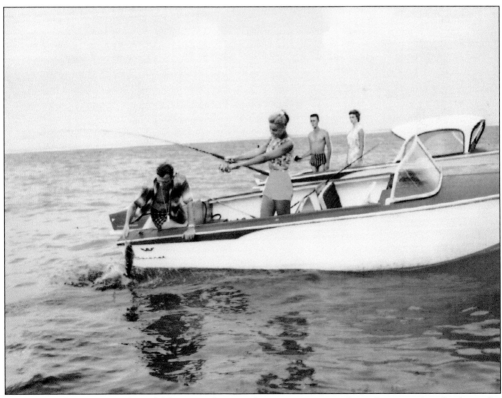

No story of Cape Coral could be complete without examining the role water has had on the community. From the Gulf of Mexico to the Caloosahatchee River and the hundreds of miles of lakes and canals, Cape Coral certainly lives up to its old "Waterfront Wonderland" moniker. Fishing, boating, and days at the beach have all been part of Cape life from the beginning.

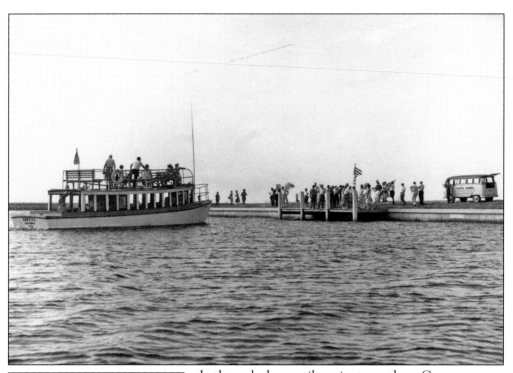

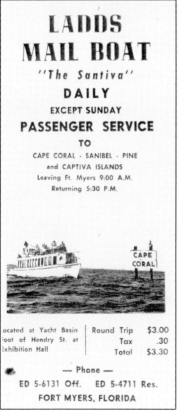

LADDS MAIL BOAT
"The Santiva"
DAILY
EXCEPT SUNDAY
PASSENGER SERVICE
TO
CAPE CORAL - SANIBEL - PINE
and CAPTIVA ISLANDS
Leaving Ft. Myers 9:00 A.M.
Returning 5:30 P.M.

ocated at Yacht Basin oot of Hendry St. at xhibition Hall	Round Trip	$3.00
	Tax	.30
	Total	$3.30

— Phone —
ED 5-6131 Off.   ED 5-4711 Res.
FORT MYERS, FLORIDA

In the early days, mail service to southern Cape Coral was quite the ordeal. The mail was picked up by boat—the *Santiva*—in Fort Myers and brought down river to the yacht basin at Cape Coral. There was not much excitement going on in Cape Coral at the time, and residents sometimes came down to the shore to watch the boat's arrival. At first, the mail was dropped off at the guard shack at Cape Coral Parkway and Del Prado Boulevard, where residents could pick it up. Later mailboxes for the entire community were set up at the Cape Coral Shopping Plaza. The *Santiva*, which was also known as Ladd's Mail Boat, also carried passengers. It was one of the few ways that people could get between Fort Myers, Cape Coral, and several of the barrier islands. The boat ran a regular schedule to Pine Island, Sanibel, and Captiva.

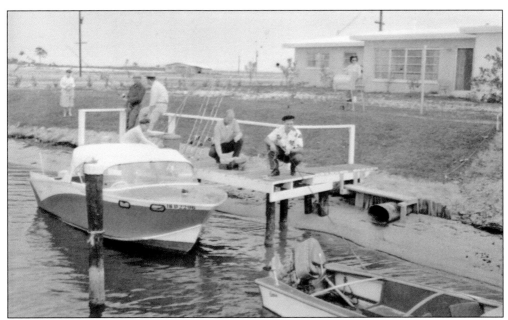

Early promotional postcards sent out across the United States play up the fabulous fishing to be found in Cape Coral. Large schools of mackerel and kingfish roamed offshore in the Gulf of Mexico. Many anglers headed to the Shell Island area just south of Cape Coral. Trout, sheepshead, and ladyfish were caught. (The ladyfish is hardly what the name implies—locals say it is a real fighter when hooked.) Redfish and the ubiquitous mullet were common catches in the backyards that lined the Cape's many saltwater canals. The postcards use lines like "a fisherman's prayer come true" and "you'll go wild when you see the redfish, snook and tarpon we pull out of our own backyards." While it is hard to imagine today, longtime residents say the Gulf and the river were teeming with fish in those early days.

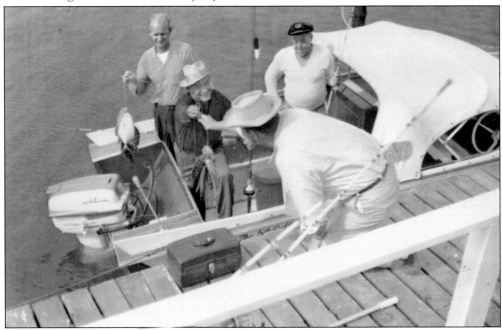

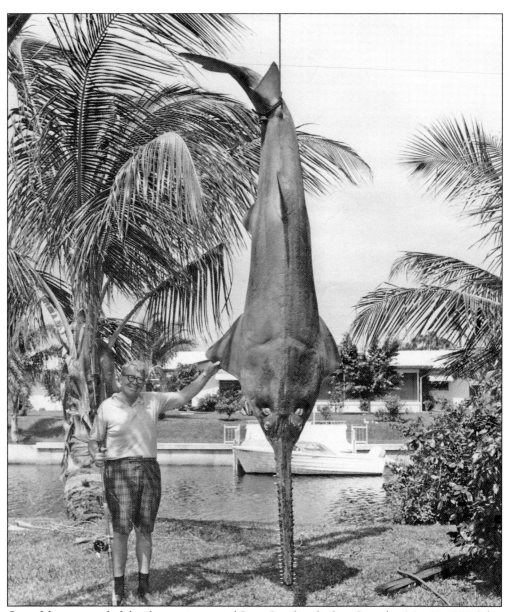

One of the great early fish tales coming out of Cape Coral took place Saturday, May 11, 1968. John Clark had gone out fishing in the Caloosahatchee River when he hooked something enormous. Clark told the local newspaper, "We had no idea of what we had on, but we knew he was big. He would surface, making a snorting noise, much like the snorting of a horse." Clark had hooked a 14-foot, 3-inch sawfish. Clark's boat was only 19 feet long, and soon the great fish was heading up the river, towing the boat behind it. Clark fought the fish for more than four hours before finally landing it. Back at his canal front home, a crane donated by a local construction firm lifted the fish off the lawn. Clark had been telling people that just a week earlier he had hooked a giant fish in the Caloosahatchee, but it got away with his wire leader. No one believed him. A week later, when Clark caught this beast, his wire leader was wrapped around its saw. The meat from the nearly 600-pound fish was donated to a local zoo, while Clark kept the 38-inch-long saw as a memento.

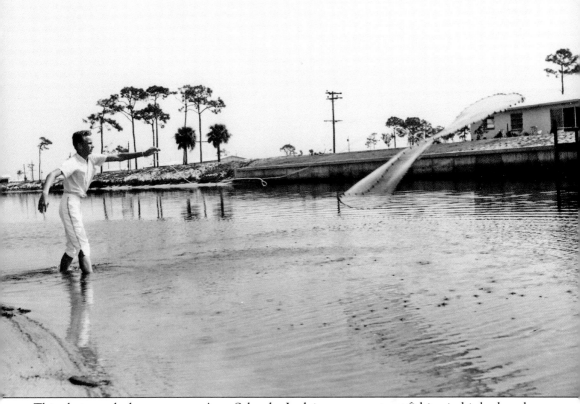

This photograph shows a young Aage Schroder Jr. doing some cast net fishing in his backyard. It was likely a promotional shot for Gulf American. Fishing with nets from the edge of a canal was a common pastime for children in Cape Coral. Mullet was the most common catch. Kids from early Cape Coral also tell of catching young snook out in the river and bringing them back to their canals, hoping to increase the snook population around their homes. Aage's younger brother, Chris, recalls regular fishing trips with his family. He says, "The fishing used to be great back then. We could go out in the Gulf and catch a hundred king mackerel in a day. I feel bad now because that's probably why there are not so many out there now." One time, Aage and his younger brothers, Leighton and Chris, caught some fish with the cast net and put them in their swimming pool. They then jumped in and tried to catch them by hand to no avail. The fish were much too fast.

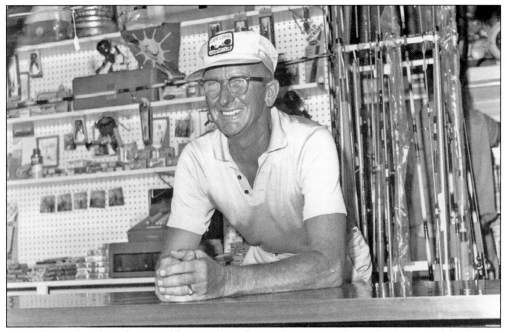

Many Cape Coral anglers would start their day with a stop at Tom Corbett's tackle shop at the yacht club pier. If they were fishing from the pier, Tom sold bait—mostly shrimp—to help fishermen land the big one. If they were headed out onto the water, he sold gas too. The shop was affectionately called the "Bait Shack."

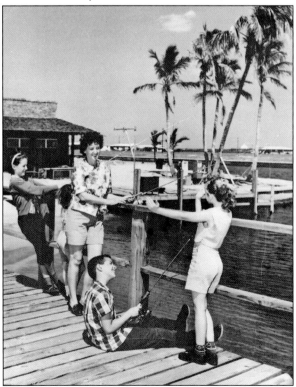

The fishing pier at the yacht club was completed in 1960. It was 12 feet wide and extended more than 600 feet into the Caloosahatchee River. It had a 200-foot T at the end. The pier was 6 feet above water, and coral and other materials were placed around it underwater to attract fish. Boaters pulling up to the pier were greeted by a sign facing out over the waters that read "Waterfront Wonderland"— Gulf American's marketing efforts covered everything.

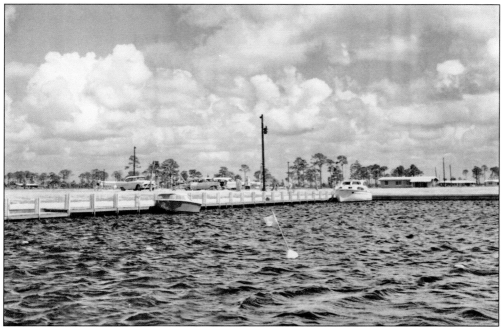

In the yacht club's early days, things were sometimes a bit slow, as evidenced by the few boats in this picture. But as the population grew, activity would pick up here, and many boats—both locals and visitors—would fill the marina. Early on, Gulf American had a tiny outboard motorboat docked here known as the *Be Back*. This little runabout was named for all the visitors to Cape Coral who said they would "be back."

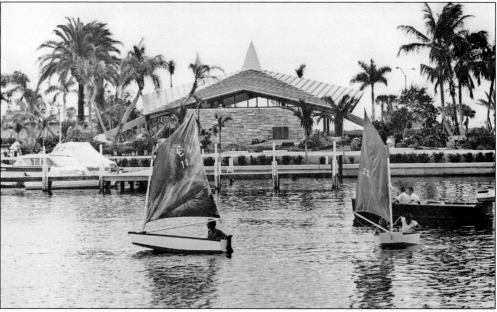

The Cape Coral Yacht Club was where many early Cape Coral residents learned how to sail, especially the children. Lessons were offered, and Gulf American, which owned the yacht club, provided small skiffs and sailboats for the children to use. Happy kids cutting wakes through the waters around Cape Coral was just the image the Rosens and their team wanted to create.

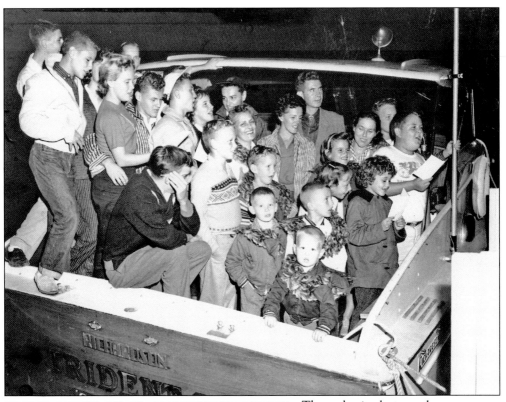

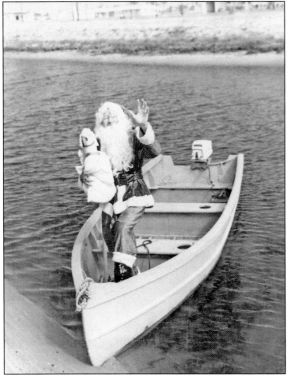

These classic photographs sum up life in early Cape Coral and how the area's waterways played a critical role. The first shows children singing Christmas carols while aboard the *Trident II* in 1959. Wally Pearson owned the *Trident II*, the boat used to take prospective homebuyers on tours. He and his wife, Irene, and their children lived in the third house built in the yacht club area. At left, there are no reindeer for this Santa Claus—he is arriving by boat. Local resident Ed McGinn, who owned the first service station in Cape Coral, was the first boat-going Santa, and none of the kids guessed who he was. When homebuilder Butch Duffala later played Santa and did some waterskiing in costume, the area's children quickly knew who was under the beard and hat. The giveaway was Duffala's unique style of waterskiing that all the kids knew.

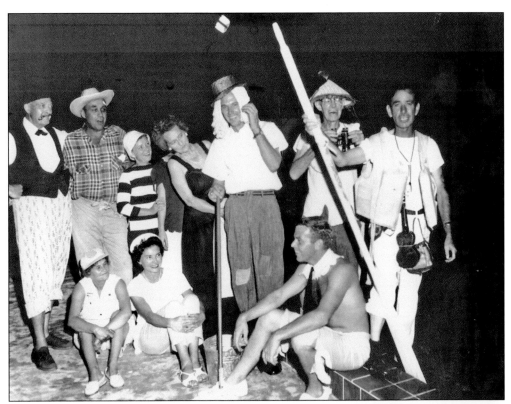

Whether it was an early morning swim or parties on the beach in the evening, the yacht club, with its pool and beach, were the center of many families' activities. These photographs show a costume party of some sort at the yacht club and the Schroder family enjoying a day at the beach. Back in the early 1960s, baseball and softball were not the main sports kids played. Rather, participating in the swimming club at the yacht club kept many children fit. The yacht club was free to all lot owners in the early years, but eventually, the population got too large to continue this, and a fence was erected.

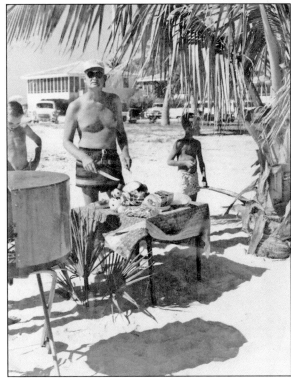

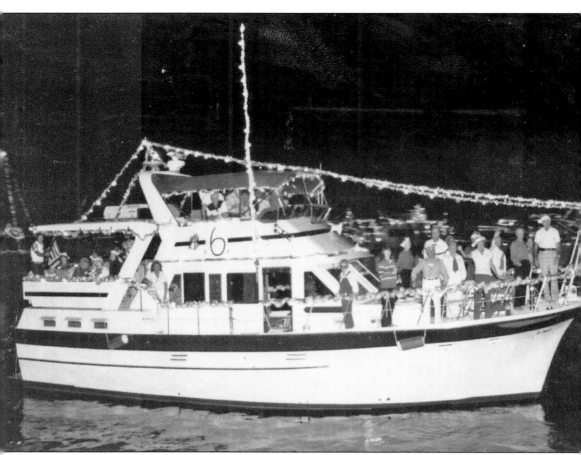

The Cape Coral Holiday Boat-A-Long is a popular tradition that started with the Deming family in 1970. The family owned a local hardware store, and one Christmas, they decided to decorate their boat with lights and music and cruise up and down neighboring canals. Their friends loved it, and the Demings did this for several years. Then, around 1974, Edwina Fox Hahn took the bull by the horns and turned the Boat-A-Long into an official city event by getting other families to participate. Boats loaded with people gather each year at the Bimini Basin at Four Freedoms Park. Vendors selling crafts and food line the waterfront, while an orchestra plays and Santa pays a visit. The Boat-A-Long tradition continues today. This 1984 photograph shows the 45-foot *Jefferson*, owned by Bud and Edie Robbins.

Eight

DAILY LIFE
BECOMING A CITY

In the first few years of Cape Coral's existence, people of every age were living in the community, with more arriving every day. There were kids—one out of three families had young children—as well as teenagers, adults, and retirees. Daily life moved at a slow, sleepy pace for many, many years. Teens often derisively called their town "Cape Coma." Nonetheless, it was a wonderful time and a close-knit community.

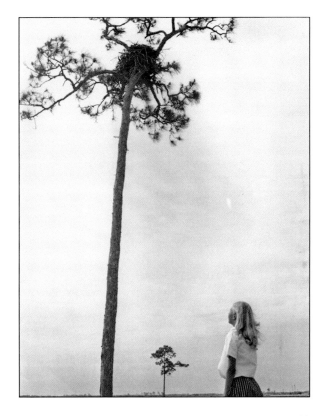

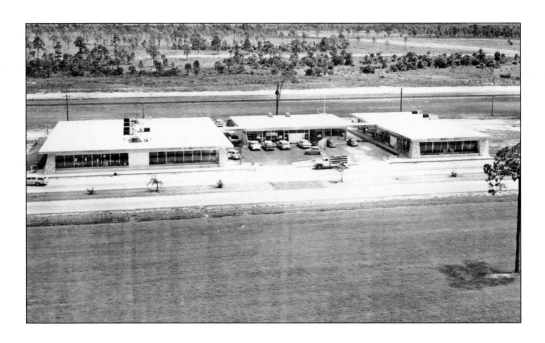

In 1960, the Cape Coral Shopping Plaza opened on the north side of Cape Coral Parkway. The community's first—and for many years only—grocery store was located there. Elmer's Market became an institution in the early Cape. The plaza also was home to Bill Smith Hardware and Appliance, a beauty and barbershop, a bakery luncheonette, a gift shop, a clothing store, and the town's first medical clinic. Today the Cape Coral Shopping Plaza is still there, although it has been greatly expanded from its earliest incarnation. It is also no longer surrounded by open fields but rather by a dense, busy downtown shopping area.

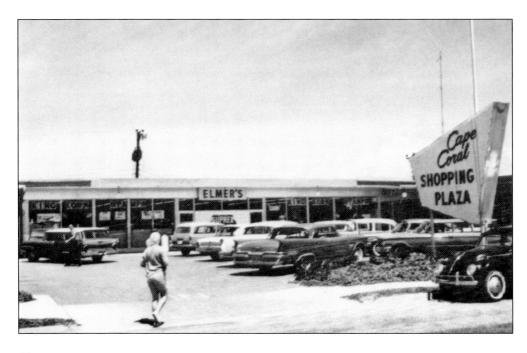

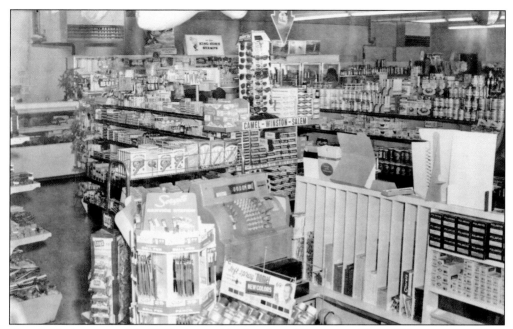

Elmer's Market opened in 1960 along with the plaza. The owner, Elmer Tabor, came to Cape Coral from West Virginia. At the time the store opened, there were only about 500 people living in the Cape. Tabor was concerned about the viability of the store and its ability to turn a profit. To that end, Gulf American agreed to subsidize the store until it could become profitable. This was both for the benefit of the current residents and a marketing tool for potential customers. Longtime residents recall that Elmer's was only open during the day; there were no evening hours like today's supermarkets. It carried a little bit of everything. In the mid-1960s, the store's name was changed to Jack's Suprex. A Publix supermarket was built nearby in 1965.

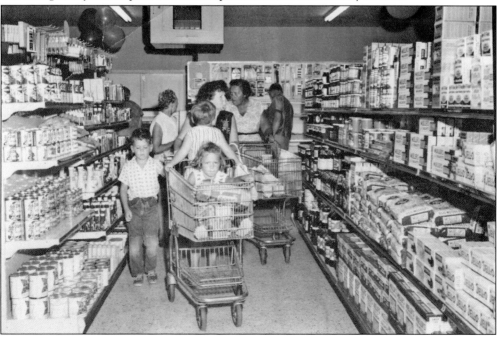

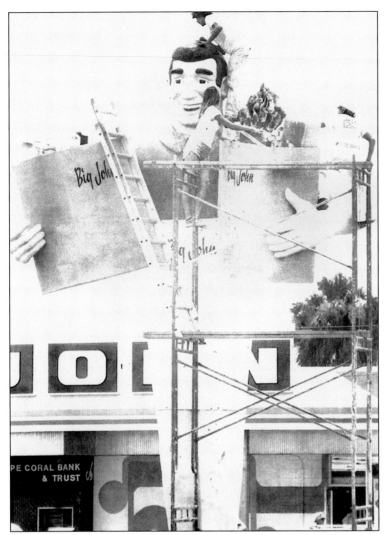

The famous Big John statue appeared in 1969, when the Hollingsworth family bought the store and renamed it Big John's. The statue was reportedly made in Illinois and traded for a semitruck full of watermelons. The statue was shipped to Cape Coral in two pieces on a truck. During the journey, the truck driver misjudged the height of an overpass and knocked off the head. It went rolling down the highway. When the pieces of Big John arrived in Cape Coral, a fiberglass specialist was flown in to repair him on the spot. The Big John statue continues to stand watch over the Cape Coral Shopping Plaza, while the eponymous supermarket closed in 1986.

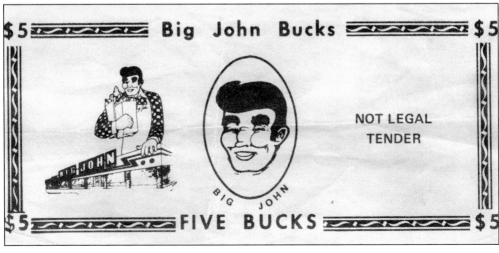

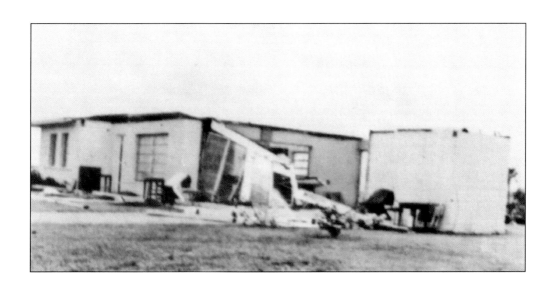

Powerful Hurricane Donna swept into Southwest Florida on September 14, 1960, and according to reports at the time, the eye passed directly over Cape Coral. Gulf American arranged for a school bus to take some residents to shelters on U.S. 41 near Fort Myers. The rest of the young Cape Coral community took refuge at the Nautilus Motel and Surfside Restaurant. Each family was given a room courtesy of the company. As the winds whipped around the buildings, time was spent mopping up water that leaked in around doors and windows. These photographs show some of the more serious damage caused by Donna to homes in Cape Coral. They come from a booklet produced in the aftermath by Joe Coleman Studios of Naples, Florida.

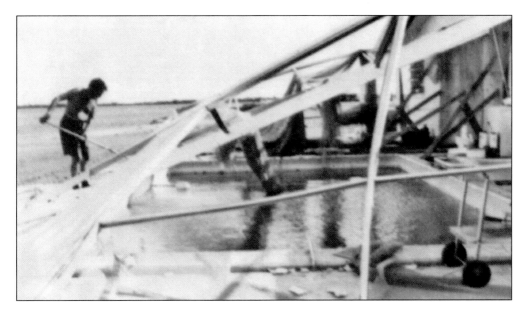

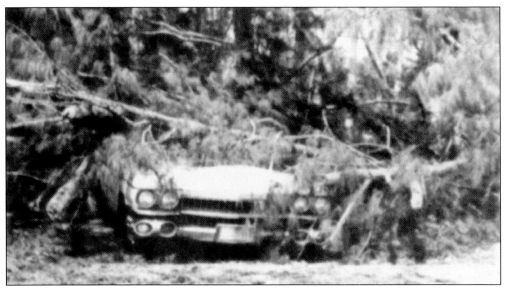

Much of the group gathered in the motel's lounge, food and drinks were served, and Henry Kurtz led a sing-a-long on the piano. As the group finished a rousing "My Old Kentucky Home," they saw it suddenly get much brighter outside. It was the eye of Hurricane Donna. Ultimately Donna did very little damage to Cape Coral. Five homes had serious damage, but most received nothing worse than torn screens and broken windows. No one was injured.

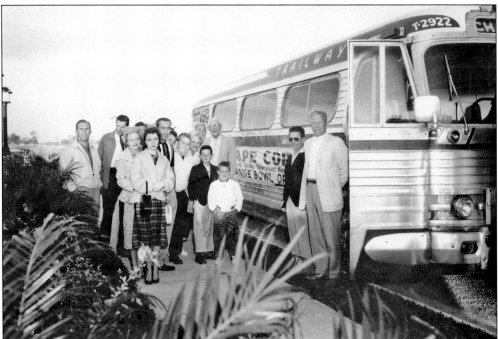

As there was little to do in Cape Coral during its earliest years, local residents were always looking for some excitement. This photograph shows a group preparing to board a Trailways bus to attend the Orange Bowl in Miami. Another photograph in the same series shows men carrying boxed lunches in old-fashioned cardboard boxes aboard the bus. The jackets the people are wearing shows that it was indeed around New Year's when this picture was snapped.

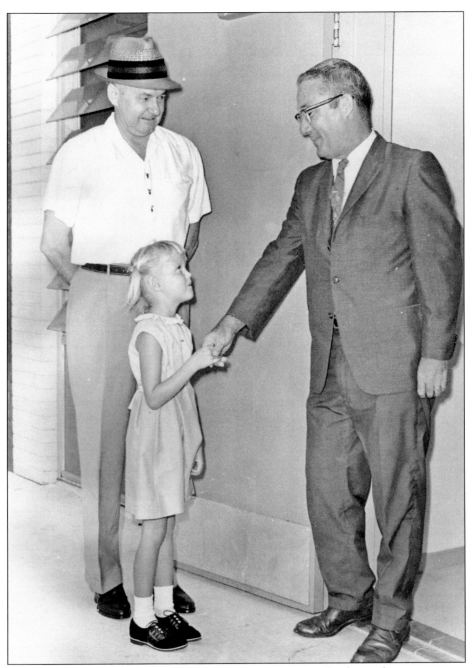

The first baby born to Cape Coral residents was Nancy Lee Loveland, seen here as a young girl. She was born on July 19, 1960, in a Fort Myers hospital. Loveland is the daughter of Adm. Kenneth Loveland (Ret.) and his wife of DeSoto Court. Nancy joined a family of two sisters—Julie Ann, 21 months, and Ann, 17 years—and a big brother, Ens. Kenneth Wilder Loveland, who was serving on the aircraft carrier *Ticonderoga* in the Far East. Nancy Lee's mother was sorry that she did not name the baby Coral after Cape Coral, but said she did not think of it until it was too late. The first baby actually born in Cape Coral (at least since the Rosens arrived) was Beth Pearson. She was born in her parents' duplex on Vincennes Street on November 18, 1966.

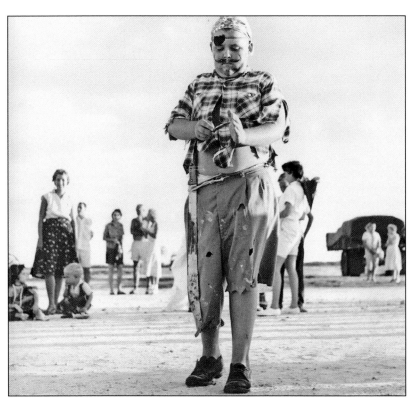

Holidays were always special times for the young community, as families and Gulf American worked hard to make them festive. Halloween time was party time in Cape Coral, as evidenced by these photographs from 1959. One shows a boy dressed as a pirate, and the other is of two boys imitating senior citizens. The odd old couple was actually Dennis Duffala and Tom Bryan, both 13. They won a dress-up contest for their creative costumes. Other early holiday activities included a Christmas party in Fort Myers, since for the first year or two, there were no restaurant or meeting facilities in the Cape. Later Santa would arrive at the community Christmas party by boat, and kids would sing carols aboard the *Trident II* as it motored up and down canals.

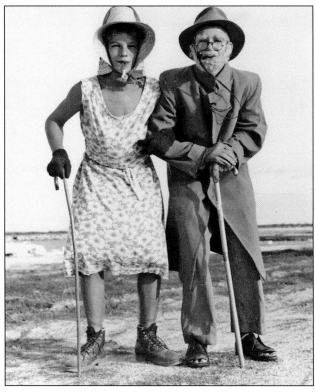

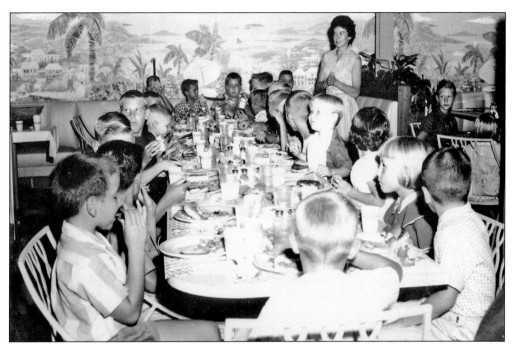

Kids' events were common in the early years of Cape Coral, such as this party for the community's children. This photograph from the early 1960s was taken during a lunch or dinner party at the Surfside Restaurant. It appears that the children are eating cheeseburgers and fries—still a favorite today. The hostess of the party, Barbara Schwartz, can be seen standing at the back of the room. She was the wife of Kenny Schwartz, Gulf American's first general manager of development.

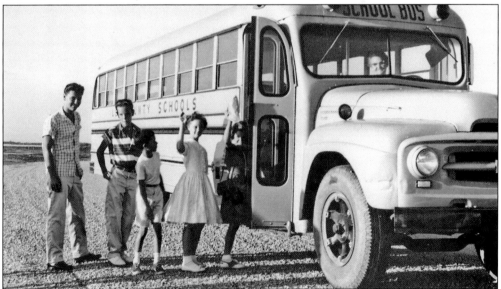

This September 1958 photograph shows the first students from Cape Coral to attend Lee County schools. From left to right are Roger Duffala, Dennis Duffala, Tommy Schwartz, Peggy Duffala, and Cheryl Simons. Chris Schroder moved to the Cape in 1959. He remembers taking the bus and the long drive up an unpaved Del Prado Boulevard. He also recalls that some boys enjoyed sticking potatoes in the exhaust pipe of the school bus, causing it to backfire.

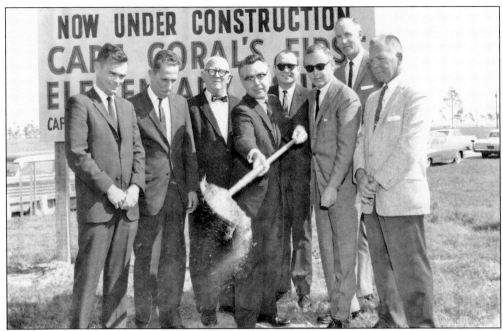

Gulf American purchased property for the first school on the Cape at 4519 Vincennes Boulevard. It cost $347,000 to build and opened in 1964. The school had 12 classrooms and six teachers for the 212 students who showed up for class on the first day. Richard Ahern was the first principal. When the school opened, part of it, including the principal's office, was still under construction. Ahern used boxes to create a makeshift desk in an unused classroom. The school grew quickly. By 1975, there were 26 classrooms, and the student population was booming.

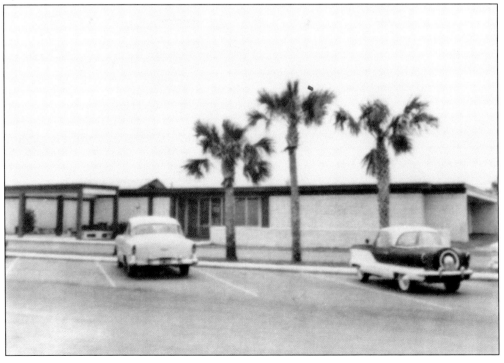

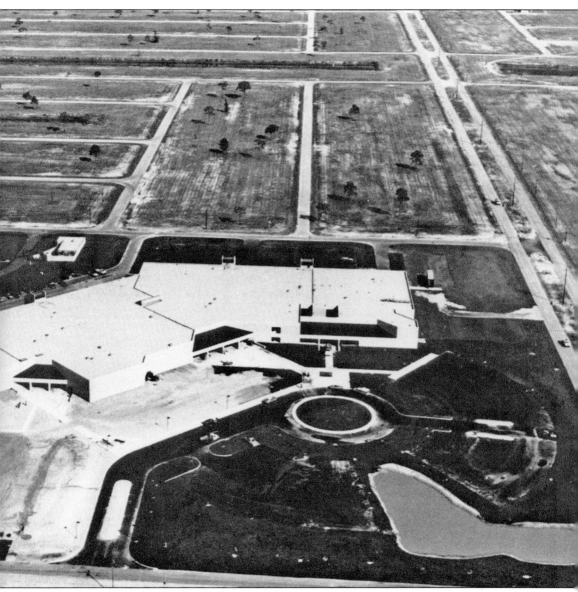

Ground was broken for the first high school in Cape Coral in 1978 on a 35-acre property on Santa Barbara Boulevard. However, delays and budget overruns prevented the $11-million school (originally budgeted at $7 million) from opening until April 14, 1980, just one month before its first senior class graduated. While they were waiting for their new school, the first students of Cape Coral High School attended other area high schools, including North Fort Myers High School and Cypress Lake High School. Approximately 1,500 students attended on opening day. There was much debate during the school's development. Some said it was a model of the school of the future, while others said it was too costly and extravagant. The school's auditorium was originally supposed to have 500 seats, but the city of Cape Coral provided additional funding and boosted the capacity to 1,000.

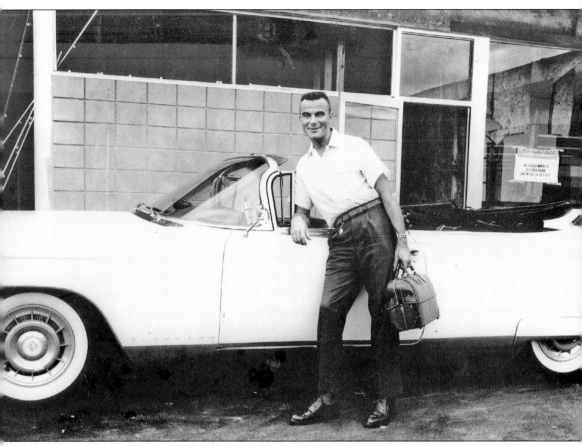

In September 1960, Dr. Theodore David (above), a Fort Myers surgeon, was encouraged to come to Cape Coral one to three days a week. Gulf American furnished him with a complete medical clinic in the Cape Coral Shopping Plaza with equipment worth $7,000. Dr. David commuted from Fort Myers to Cape Coral by boat and was known to fish along the way. With more than 2,000 residents in Cape Coral by 1962, it was time to have a full-time doctor. Dr Robert R. Tate, a young physician looking to set up a practice and already a Cape home site owner, was located. Tate opened his office on August 27, 1962, with the promise that Gulf American would guarantee his income for the first year. As of today, Dr. Tate is still in practice at his office on Del Prado Boulevard, nearly five decades after he opened his practice.

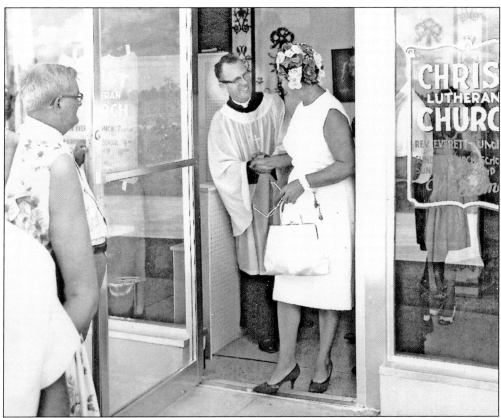

The first known religious services in Cape Coral were held in the lounge at the Nautilus Motel by the Reverend Henry Dickert, a retired Lutheran minister. Rev. Everett Bunck was the first to have his own place when he conducted Lutheran services in a storefront church in the Cape Coral Shopping Plaza. The first church built in Cape Coral was the Faith United Presbyterian Church on Coronado Parkway. It was dedicated in February 1964 and is still there and tending to its flock to this day. Rather than drive 30 to 40 miles round-trip to Fort Myers to attend a church of their own faith, longtime residents recall that many early Cape Coral residents became temporary Presbyterians. By 1966, there were six churches and one synagogue on the Cape.

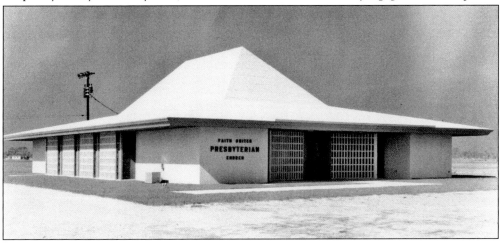

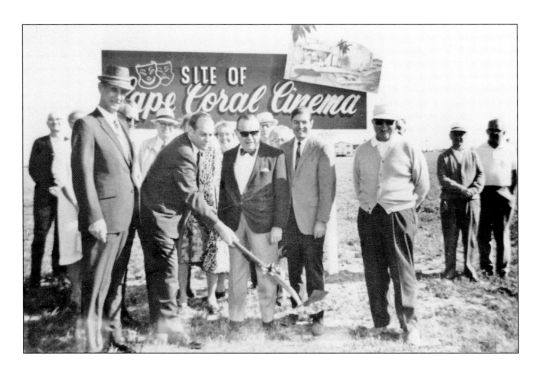

A long-held dream was realized when plans developed to bring a movie theater to Cape Coral. Plans were announced in 1968, and the $250,000 building opened in 1970. The Cape Coral Cinema was located between Forty-seventh Street and Forty-seventh Terrace, east of Del Prado Boulevard. It had 850 seats, and the first movie shown there was the Academy Award–winning *Patton*, starring George C. Scott. Florida governor Claude Kirk was campaigning in the area and attended a ribbon-cutting ceremony at the new movie house. Today the former Cape Coral Cinema building is a church. The photograph above shows the groundbreaking ceremony. Below is an early artist's rendering of what the cinema would look like.

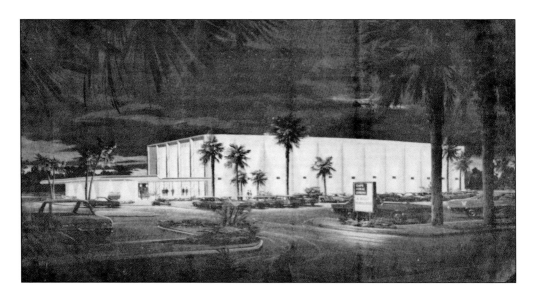

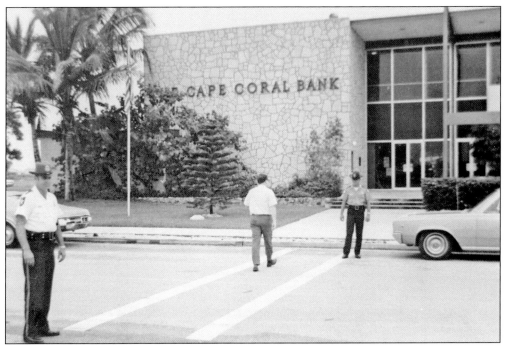

Cape Coral Bank, later known as Sun Bank Southwest, was the first bank to open in Cape Coral. Lowell Mills came to the Cape in 1958 and intended to enjoy his retirement until he saw the need for a bank in the growing community of 214 people. At the time, the closest bank was in Fort Myers, a 28-mile round-trip via the old Route 41 bridge. Mills and a few of his fellow retired businessmen rallied around the idea, and Mills traveled to Tallahassee to work out the details for a charter. The bank opened in early 1964.

The newspapers of the day were filled with notices for early Cape Coral businesses. This one is from Robert's Cape Coral Pharmacy wishing the community a Happy New Year. Note that there is no address for the business. Many of the advertisements did not feature addresses, because everyone knew where they were. Others included Wonderland Realty, Iverson's Furniture, Sunshine Movers, Pankow Plumbing, Sun 'n' Surf, Willy's Restaurant, Glardon's Custom Cut Meats, and the Shop Rite Food Store.

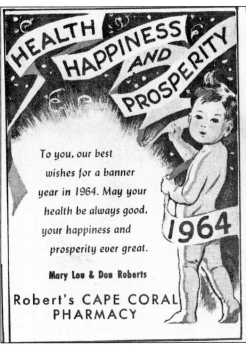

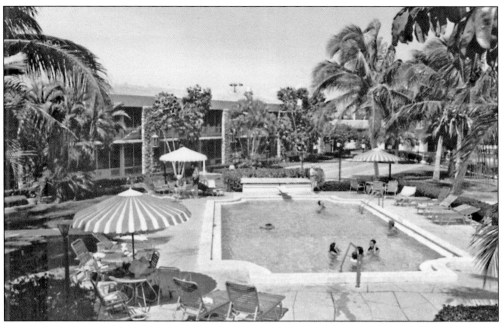

Besides the famed Nautilus Motel (later Congress Inn), other early motels came into Cape Coral to serve the growing population of both residents and tourists. The Del Prado Inn was originally built by Gulf American to house the influx of visitors, and later was affiliated with the Best Western chain. It was located at Del Prado Boulevard and Miramar Street. It featured 100 rooms, a restaurant, and a swimming pool. Today it is still a motel, although not the Del Prado.

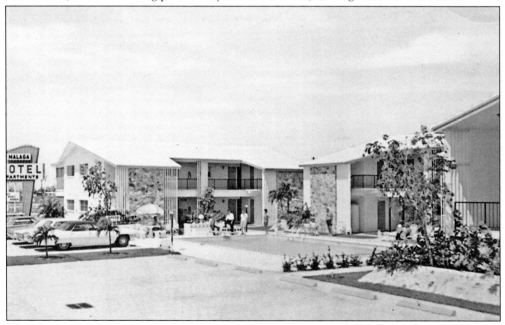

The Malaga Motel, another early inn, is seen in this 1960s postcard. It offered efficiencies as well as one- and two-bedroom suites. It boasted central heat and air-conditioning as well as televisions, a swimming pool, and a private boat dock. The guest rooms of the Malaga Motel still stand, but they are now private apartments.

People moved to Cape Coral from locations across the United States and even from around the world, especially Europe. One should not underestimate the importance of local clubs and community groups that sprang up in Cape Coral's first decade. They proved critical in helping people make friends and find their place in the rapidly growing Cape. Many clubs had to do with a home state, such as the Buckeye Club for Ohio natives. Others had to do with hobbies, such as the Orchid Club, a member of which is seen in the photograph at right. One of the most well-known clubs in Cape Coral is the German-American Club. Members are seen below in 1966. The club was formed by Willy Gruetzenbach to help the Cape's large German population get used to a new country and a new climate. The club is most famous now for its annual Oktoberfest celebrations that attract visitors from around the state.

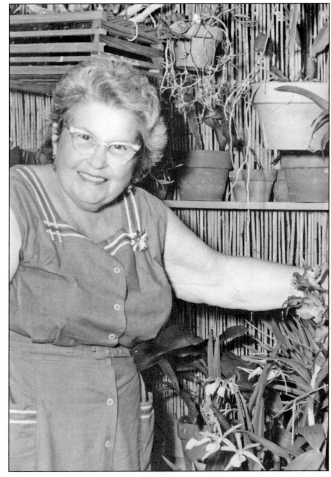

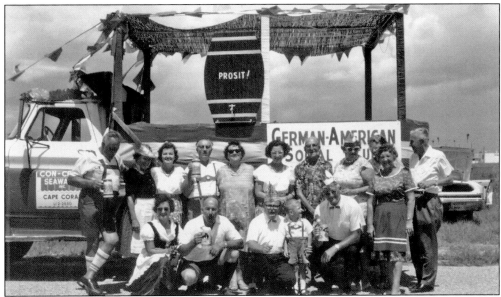

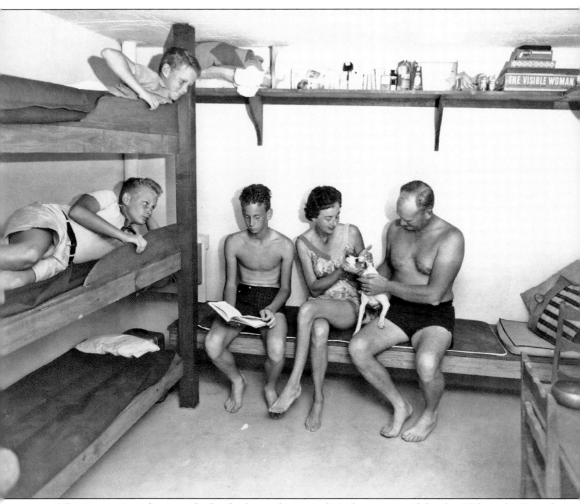

This interesting photograph clearly shows the geopolitical concerns of the day. When the Bay of Pigs invasion in Cuba raised tensions between the United States and Cuba, John Holmes and Aage Schroder decided to build fallout shelters at their Cape Coral homes. As the Cape is a waterfront wonderland, Schroder's family recalls he could only dig down about 3 feet before hitting water. Thus this shelter was partially in the ground and partially above the ground. Its walls were heavy duty—2 feet of concrete followed by 2 feet of dirt and then 2 more feet of concrete. The family stocked it with food and ran occasional practice drills. Later Schroder's son, Chris, used the shelter as a dark room for his photography. The thick structure got somewhat damp and moldy inside and went unused, even for storage, for the next 30 years or so. When Aage Schroder went to sell the home, a creative real estate agent tried to list the shelter as a wine cellar. The shelter still sits on the side of the old Schroder house today.

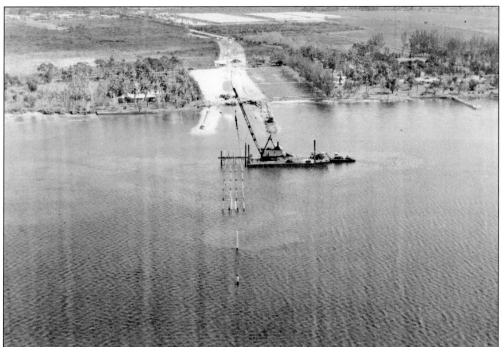

Early Cape Coral residents had a long trip ahead of them to get to Fort Myers—nearly 20 miles through North Fort Myers. This was the justification to build a bridge in the early 1960s. Still, the county was hesitant. Officials worried that there would not be enough traffic and that tolls collected would not cover the bond payments. Once again, Leonard Rosen stepped in. He put $100,000 in escrow and said anytime traffic did not generate enough money, the rest due could be taken from the account. It was never needed, as traffic was sufficient. Rosen got his money back. Before transponders in car windows, regular bridge users were issued booklets of tickets to cross the Cape Coral Bridge. The total length of the Cape Coral Bridge is 3,400 feet, and the vertical clearance is 55 feet.

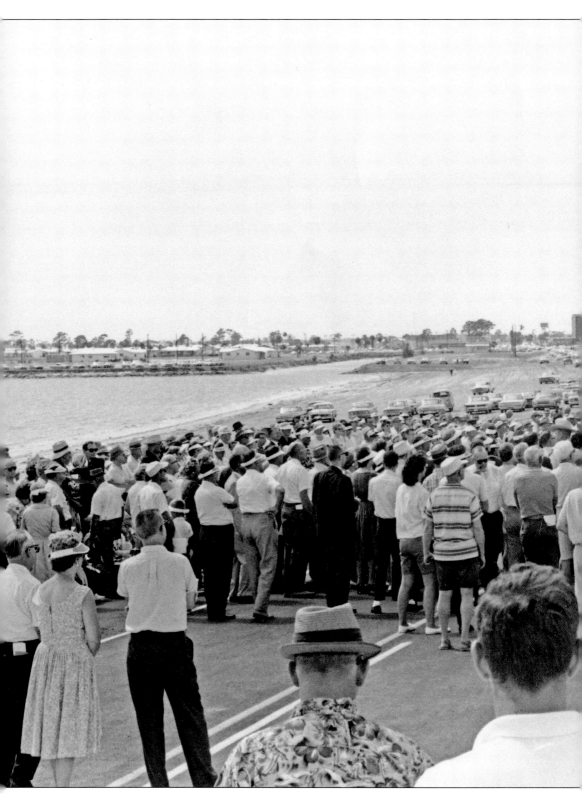

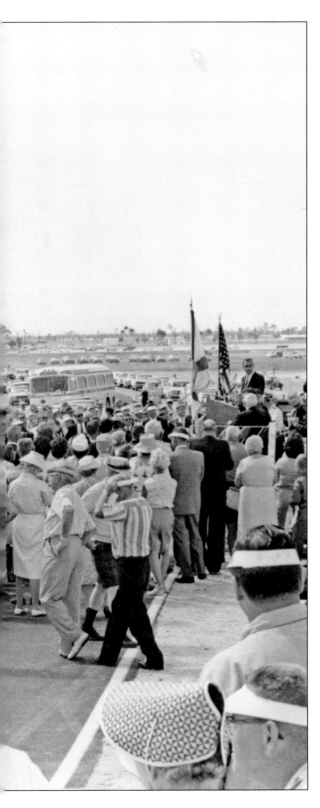

The Cape Coral Bridge span opened on March 14, 1964, at 9:30 a.m. with one lane in each direction. This photograph was taken at the bridge's dedication a year later. In 1989, a second parallel span was constructed for eastbound traffic with the original span being used for westbound traffic. Within a few years, debate began over whether another bridge was needed. For 20 years, the discussion raged. Much of the arguing had to do with concerns that the approach to Fort Myers would destroy historic McGregor Boulevard. Finally, in 1997, the Midpoint Memorial Bridge was opened, giving Cape Coral residents a direct shot to Interstate 75. The total cost for the 1.25-mile-long bridge was $174 million. Interestingly, the original engineers of the Cape Coral Bridge argued that it should be built further north—in the exact spot that the Midpoint Memorial Bridge stands today. However, the Rosen brothers argued that no one lived that far north.

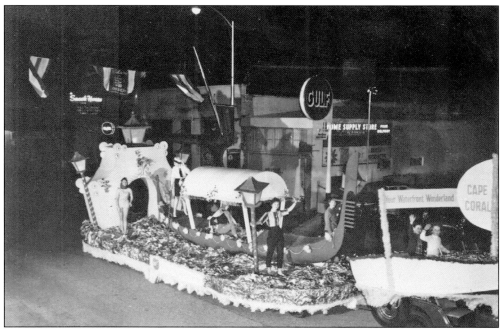

No self-respecting Lee County community would dare not have a presence in the Edison Pageant of Light Parade in Fort Myers. This grande dame of local events is held each winter. This photograph shows Cape Coral's first float in the parade from either 1959 or 1960. It features an Italian gondola, playing off the Cape's reputation for grand canals like the ones in Venice.

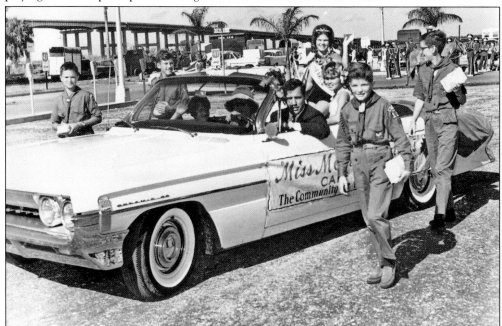

Little is known about this photograph, which shows Miss Merry Christmas, a Cape Coral beauty queen title. This parade took place in Fort Myers. While no one has been able to identify Miss Merry Christmas herself, the names of the Boy Scouts walking next to her royal car are known. They are, from left to right, Andy Garrow, Duane Seger, Bobby Baumann, and Louis Benson.

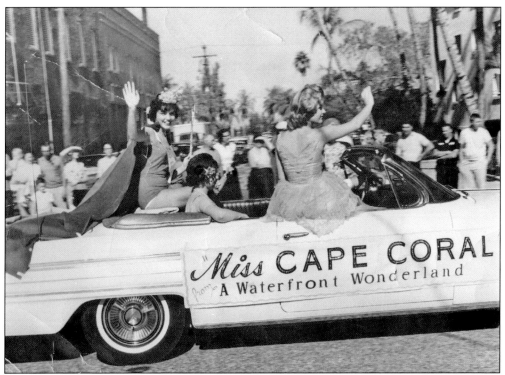

Back in the mid-20th century, beauty pageants were a beloved part of American culture used for scholarships and publicity. The Cape Coral Chamber of Commerce got in on the action by sponsoring an annual Miss Cape Coral pageant. The first winner was Roberta "Bobbi" Blackwell, who took the title in 1962 and is seen riding in a local parade. The program for young women was reportedly completely local and not connected to any of the state or national pageant programs. The second photograph features yet another parade and another Miss Cape Coral. Based on the sign on the side of the car, Sally Bendroth was apparently Miss Cape Coral 1967.

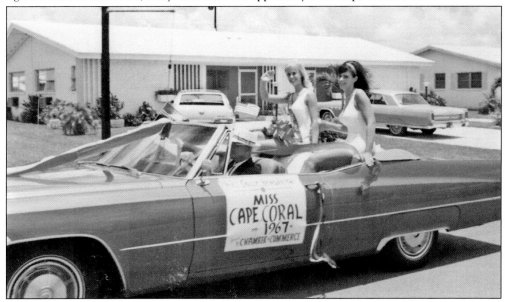

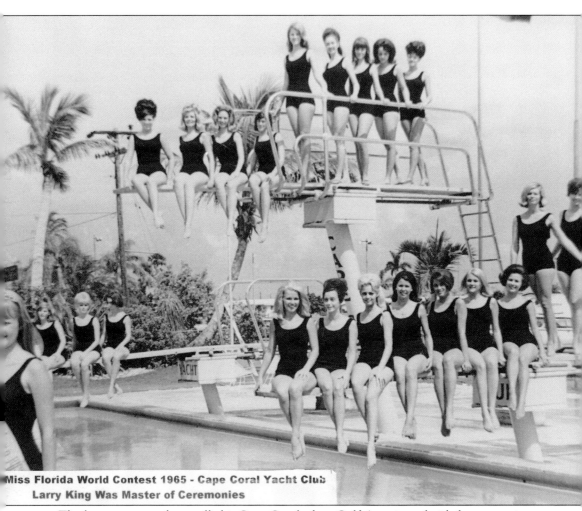

Miss Florida World Contest 1965 - Cape Coral Yacht Club
Larry King Was Master of Ceremonies

The beauty pageant bug really bit Cape Coral when Gulf American decided to create its own pageant as another promotional vehicle to promote the community. The name of the pageant was Miss Florida World, and there is some debate over how many years it was held. This photograph comes from 1965. Dozens of gorgeous women came from all over Florida and descended on the Cape Coral Yacht and Racquet Club for the event. A stage and runway rimmed with light bulbs was built out over the pool. Well-known television talk show host Larry King was a young radio broadcaster in Miami at the time. The Rosens paid him $1,500 to come to Cape Coral and emcee the pageant. The first Miss Florida World crowned in the Cape was Lanita Kent in 1963. According to the International Movie Database, Kent went on to have some small roles on television, including *The Jackie Gleason Show* of the late 1960s. Carole Hale, a Cape Coral native, won the pageant in 1964. Mary Anna Duncan from South Miami won in 1965.

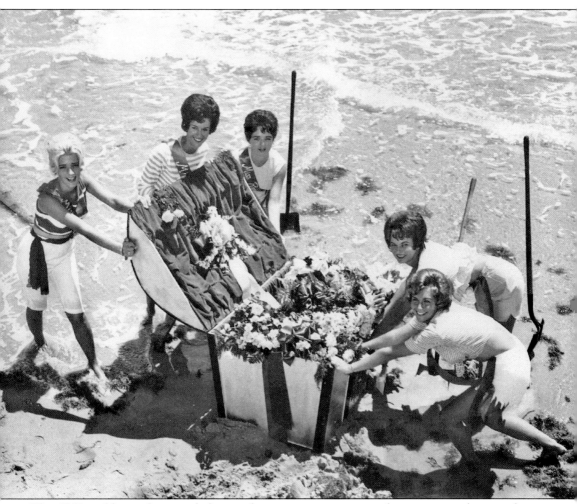

This 1960s publicity photograph features beauty queens opening a large treasure chest on the beach only to discover it filled with flowers. It was part of a press release touting the region's flower power in the horticultural industry. During the decade, 75 percent of all U.S. gladioli and 60 percent of the country's pompon chrysanthemums were grown in Florida. Each winter and spring, the state would send more than eight million gladiolus shipments and more than one million pompons to points north. At the time, there were gladiolus farms in Cape Coral on Pine Island Road, Burnt Store Road, and Del Prado Boulevard. The largest flower farm was the Gulf Coast Farm on Pine Island Road across from the German-American Club. The 4,000-acre farm raised cattle as well as flowers.

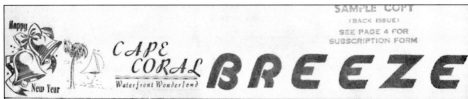

A number of papers have covered the news in Cape Coral. The most well known is the *Cape Coral Breeze*, which has served the people of Cape Coral since it was first published in December 1961 as a weekly. The paper became a semi-weekly in 1974 and a daily in 1975. Other newspapers published over the years include the *Cape Coral Times* and the *Cape Coral Sun*, both published in the early 1960s, and the *Cape Coral Pointer*, published in the 1980s.

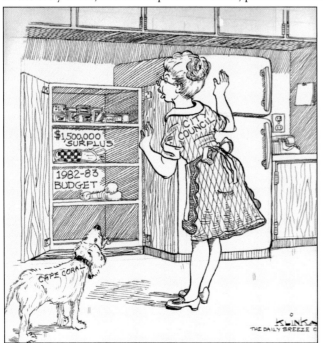

The *Cape Coral Breeze* has been lucky enough to have some very skilled political cartoonists over the years. Ed Klinka was one. He drew insightful single-panel cartoons that poked fun at the foibles of life in Cape Coral and especially the city's sometimes-tenuous relationship with greater Lee County. A large number of his original cartoons, as well as those by other cartoonists, were donated to the Cape Coral Historical Museum.

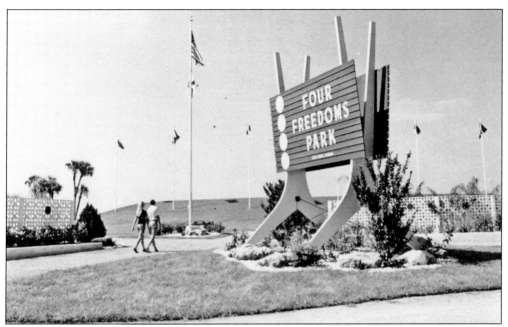

The first park in Cape Coral was created by Gulf American and named the Four Freedoms Park. The park's name comes from a speech given by Pres. Franklin Delano Roosevelt in 1941. The "Four Freedoms" were freedom of speech and expression, freedom to worship, freedom from want, and freedom from fear. Franklin D. Roosevelt Jr. was a guest at the park's dedication in 1964. The park sign, seen in this photograph, was originally the sign at the Nautilus Motel on Cape Coral Parkway. It is now long gone.

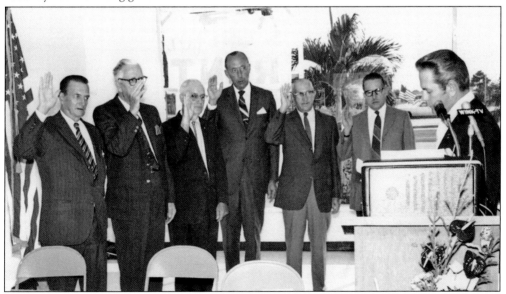

Early on, many residents of Cape Coral realized that one day their community would need to leave the comfortable bosom of Gulf American and stand on its own. To this end, the Cape Coral Civic Association was formed in 1962. The community organization was instrumental in guiding the city towards incorporation. In 1970, by a referendum of the people, Cape Coral became a city. It chose a city council–city manager form of government. The first mayor was Paul Fickinger.

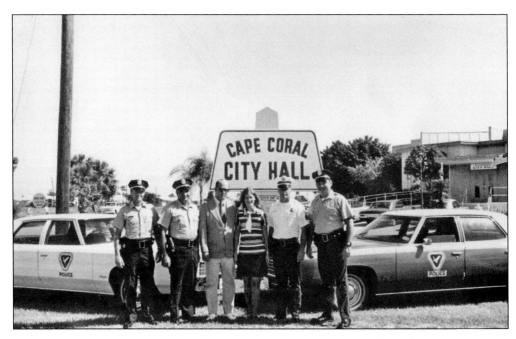

When the city was incorporated in 1970, a city police department was formally established. The force was made up of Chief Jim White, a lieutenant, two officers, and a secretary. The department was housed in the city hall building, and it had just two patrol cars. In the July 1971 photograph above are, from left to right, patrolman Gordon Shute, patrolman Andy Costa, Chief Jim White, secretary Barbara Cole, Sgt. Bill Gilmore, and patrolman Bernie Schwartz. With some 400 miles of canals in Cape Coral, an official police boat is a must. Below is the Cape's first in 1972 with patrolmen Renny Wiersman (left) and Andy Costa.

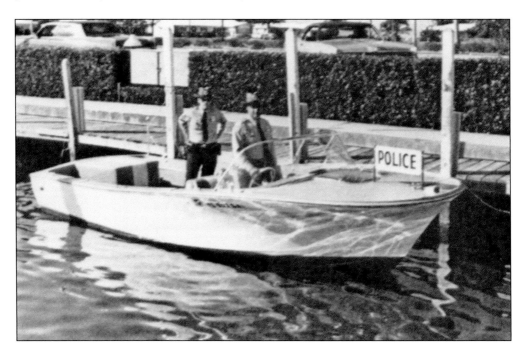

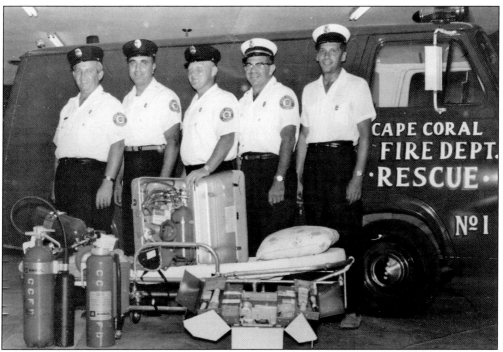

In 1961, Cape Coral residents decided that they wanted their own fire department. It took far too long for fire trucks from North Fort Myers to drive all the way down Del Prado Boulevard to respond to alarms. By 1962, a fire board had been established to oversee the start of a department. Gulf American agreed to match dollar for dollar up to $5,000. The company also donated land at Chester and Lafayette Streets for a fire station. Cape households were asked to contribute $10 each towards the department. The Cape Coral Teen Club was one of the first groups to organize and raise funds. The young people made a $100 donation.

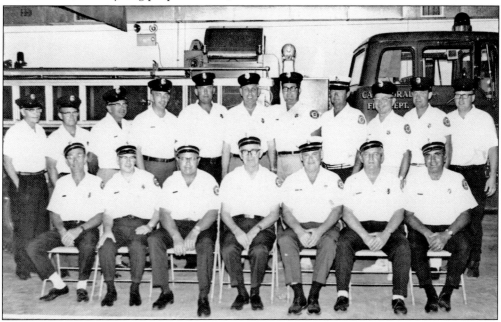

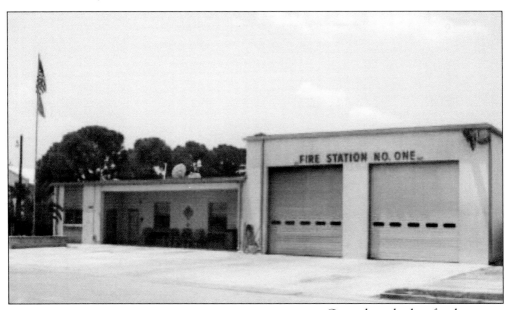

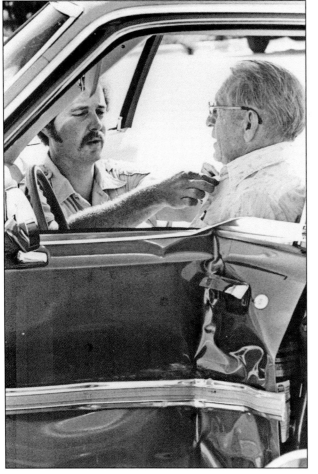

Ground was broken for the Chester Street station in October 1962. Perhaps to drum up business, a Fort Myers funeral home donated an ambulance to the all-volunteer fire department. The station opened in 1963, and many meetings and special events were held there. However, it was not until 1964 that Cape Coral got its first fire truck. It was a John Beam Class A Pumper and cost $24,000. After the city's incorporation in 1970, the fire board was dissolved, and the fire department became part of the city. Tim Herrick was the department's first paid fire chief.

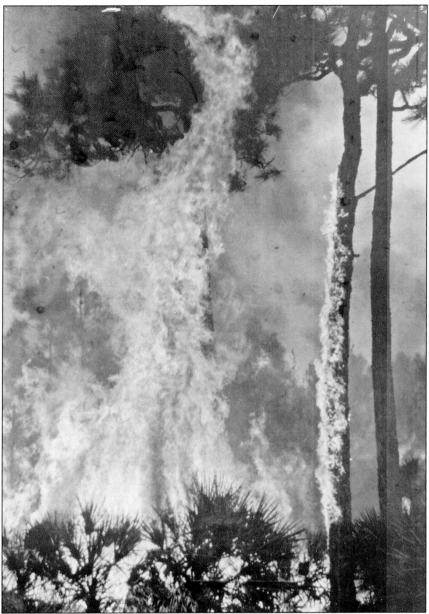

In the Cape's earliest years, the volunteer firemen were always ready. At least one firefighter would stay at the station. When an emergency call came in, this lone sentry would use the bar phone, which allowed him to dial one number and reach all the firefighters' homes at once. He would relay the nature of the emergency and the location, then run outside, ring the siren to alert others, and take the fire truck to the scene. Meanwhile, the first person who answered the bar phone would stay on the line and let everyone else know where to go as they answered the call. Another interesting aspect of early Cape Coral is that ambulance services were often handled by funeral homes. When a Cape Coral resident needed to be rushed to the hospital, the town's ambulance would sometimes meet a funeral home ambulance in North Fort Myers and pass the patient off for the remainder of the journey to Lee Memorial Hospital. Later funeral homes located in the Cape offered ambulance services as well.

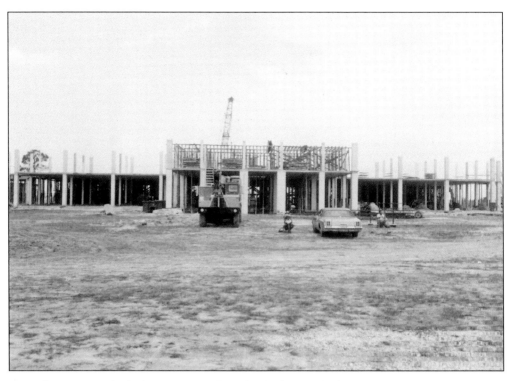

Dr. Robert R. Tate built the Cape Coral Medical Clinic, which opened in 1965 on Coronado Parkway. He and Dr. Wallace Dawson had been practicing in a small office in the shopping plaza on Cape Coral Parkway. In the early 1970s, it was sold to the city for a library, and they built the medical clinic on Del Prado Boulevard. Eventually, Dr. Tate and some friends formed a hospital board of directors with Connie Mack as chairman, and the Cape Coral Hospital became a reality. Some 500 people attended the grand opening of the new $8.5-million facility in June 1977. The hospital's first patient came a few days later, when Violet Barone arrived seeking treatment for a fishhook that had gotten lodged in her scalp.

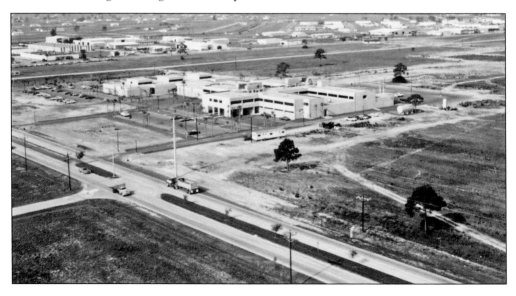

Over the years, Cape Coral's permanent population has grown rapidly. According to historical society records, there were approximately five families calling the Cape home in 1950. By 1960, two years after the Rosens and Gulf American began building their dream, the population was 280. In 1970, it reached 11,470, and it nearly tripled to 32,103 by 1980. In 1990, 74,991 people lived in Cape Coral. This jumped to 102,206 in 2000 and climbed again to an estimated 170,000 residents in 2007.

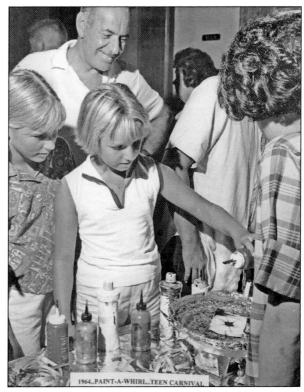

1964..PAINT-A-WHIRL..TEEN CARNIVAL

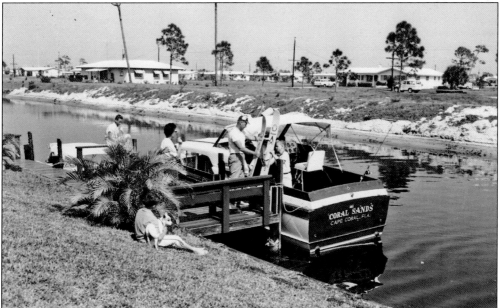

Cape Coral's statistics are extreme. Besides the tremendous jumps in population over the decades, other numbers tell the city's tale. According to records, there are 105 miles of saltwater canals and another 295 miles of freshwater canals. Anyone who has driven in the Cape knows these many waterways make for countless dead end roads. To help motorists navigate this Waterfront Wonderland, Cape Coral had 156 bridges as of 2008.

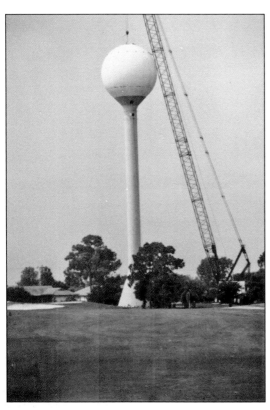

One of Cape Coral's most famous landmarks was the golf tee water tower near the Cape Coral Country Club, pictured on its final day in these never-before-seen snapshots. The giant tank was built in the early 1960s to supply water to the new community. Due to its proximity to the course, the decision was made to paint the top white like an enormous golf ball and make the tower portion resemble a tee. This design proved to be invaluable to lost drivers for years, as it stood out clearly on Cape Coral's flat horizon and helped people orient themselves and find their destinations.

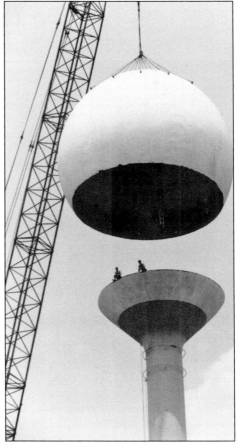

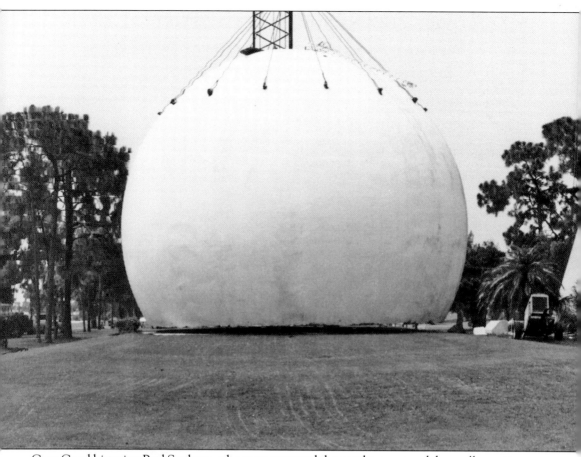

Cape Coral historian Paul Sanborn, who once managed the nearby country club, recalls one time in the early 1970s when a big, burly golfer lined up and drove the ball so far (at least 400 yards) that it bounced off the side of the tank. When the decision was made in the 1980s to remove the old tower, many Cape Coral residents fought the move. Nonetheless, it was disassembled, as captured in these historic photographs. Some might say with it went the old Cape Coral—the city that rose from a dream and a woody peninsula. In its place stood a major, modern city moving into the future with the same unique style and outlook that made it famous so many decades ago.

About the Organization

The Cape Coral Historical Society was founded in 1978 to record, preserve, and display the unique history of Cape Coral. The society operates a large, three-building museum campus on Cultural Park Boulevard, including a historic 1960s building that was once part of the original golf pro shop and snack bar at the Cape Coral Country Club. The museum features a reference library and archive, a memorial rose garden, two buildings filled with displays on the area's history, and a gift shop. The society sponsors monthly speaker's presentations, annual field trips, and special group tours. The Cape Coral Historical Society members invite you to join them in their mission.

Discover Thousands of Local History Books Featuring Millions of Vintage Images

Arcadia Publishing, the leading local history publisher in the United States, is committed to making history accessible and meaningful through publishing books that celebrate and preserve the heritage of America's people and places.

Find more books like this at
www.arcadiapublishing.com

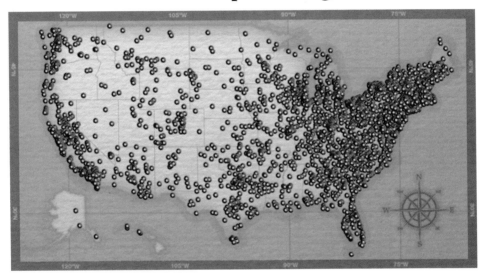

Search for your hometown history, your old stomping grounds, and even your favorite sports team.

Consistent with our mission to preserve history on a local level, this book was printed in South Carolina on American-made paper and manufactured entirely in the United States. Products carrying the accredited Forest Stewardship Council (FSC) label are printed on 100 percent FSC-certified paper.

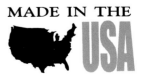